PASTA

BARNES
& NOBLE
BOOKS

NEW YORK

Pictured on front cover:

Trattoria-Style Fettuccine, *page 16*

Previously published as
Better Homes and Gardens® Cooking for Today Pasta

Copyright © 2004, 1993 by Meredith Corporation, Des Moines, Iowa. First Edition.

This edition published for Barnes & Noble, Inc., by Meredith Books.

Printed in China

ISBN: 0-7607-6037-3

Dress it up or play it down. Pasta offers endless possibilities for a fine dining experience, a quick family supper, and every meal in-between. What other food combines so deliciously with beef, pork, seafood, and chicken, not to mention many vegetables? And the sauce possibilities are just as varied—rich cream sauces, spicy tomato sauces, and garlicky butter sauces.

Among the recipes on these pages, you will find strands of linguine tossed with an Oriental-flavored peanut sauce, tube-shaped mostaccioli baked in a casserole with chicken and a peppery cheese sauce, tiny ditalini cooked with sausage in a smokey-scented soup, and colorful pasta twists chilled with beef and artichoke hearts for a refreshing main-dish salad.

To explore the endless possibilities and enjoy the versatile good taste of pasta, simply turn the pages and choose a dish that fills the bill for dinner tonight.

CONTENTS

FUSILLI WITH CREAMY TOMATO AND MEAT SAUCE

Whipping cream enriches this herbed tomato and meat sauce. Serve it over your favorite pasta strands.

12 ounces ground beef *or* ground raw
       turkey
 1 large onion, chopped (1 cup)
 2 cloves garlic, minced
 2 14-ounce cans peeled Italian-style
       tomatoes, cut up
 1 teaspoon dried Italian seasoning,
       crushed
 ½ teaspoon sugar
 ¼ teaspoon salt
 ⅛ teaspoon pepper
 8 ounces packaged dried fusilli,
       vermicelli, *or* spaghetti
 ½ cup whipping cream
 2 tablespoons snipped parsley
       Fresh rosemary sprigs (optional)

For sauce, in a large saucepan cook beef or turkey, onion, and garlic till meat is brown. Drain fat. Stir in *undrained* tomatoes, Italian seasoning, sugar, salt, and pepper. Bring to boiling; reduce heat. Simmer, uncovered, about 40 minutes or till most of liquid has evaporated, stirring occasionally.

Meanwhile, cook pasta according to the directions on page 140. Drain; keep warm.

Gradually stir the whipping cream into the sauce. Heat through, stirring constantly. Remove from heat. Stir in parsley.

Arrange the pasta on individual plates or a large platter. Spoon the sauce over the pasta. If desired, garnish with fresh rosemary sprigs. Makes 4 main-dish servings.

Nutrition information per serving: 523 calories, 26 g protein, 59 g carbohydrate, 21 g fat (10 g saturated), 94 mg cholesterol, 534 mg sodium, 783 mg potassium.

BEEF STRIPS WITH VERMICELLI

Strips of top round steak make a lean choice for this sauce whether you are counting calories or pennies.

8 ounces boneless beef top round steak
4 ounces packaged dried vermicelli *or* spaghetti
1 tablespoon cooking oil
1 medium onion, chopped (½ cup)
1 16-ounce can tomato wedges
1 9-ounce package frozen Italian-style green beans *or* cut green beans
1 4-ounce can sliced mushrooms, drained
½ of a 6-ounce can (⅓ cup) Italian-style tomato paste
½ teaspoon fennel seed, crushed (optional)
¼ teaspoon pepper
1 tablespoon grated Parmesan cheese
   Grated Parmesan cheese (optional)

Partially freeze meat. Trim fat from meat. Thinly slice meat across the grain into bite-size strips.

Cook pasta according to the directions on page 140. Drain; keep warm.

Meanwhile, for sauce, heat oil in a large skillet over medium-high heat. Add meat and onion. Stir-fry for 2 to 3 minutes or till meat is brown.

Stir in *undrained* tomato wedges, green beans, mushrooms, tomato paste, fennel seed (if desired), and pepper. Bring to boiling; reduce heat. Simmer, uncovered, for 7 to 8 minutes or till slightly thickened, stirring frequently. Stir in Parmesan cheese.

Arrange pasta on individual plates or a large platter. Spoon the sauce over pasta. If desired, sprinkle with additional Parmesan cheese. Makes 4 main-dish servings.

Nutrition information per serving: 278 calories, 18 g protein, 38 g carbohydrate, 7 g fat (2 g saturated), 28 mg cholesterol, 488 mg sodium, 729 mg potassium.

HAM AND PASTA WITH MUSHROOM-CHEESE SAUCE

Make dinner easy on yourself. Buy the cut-up vegetables from your grocery store's salad bar and pick up a package of shredded cheese.

6 ounces packaged dried spinach *and/or* plain linguine
2 medium carrots, cut into ½-inch pieces (1 cup)
1 cup broccoli flowerets
1 cup sliced fresh mushrooms
2 tablespoons margarine *or* butter
2 tablespoons all-purpose flour
1 tablespoon snipped parsley
½ teaspoon dried basil, crushed
1¼ cups milk
6 ounces sliced fully cooked ham, cut into bite-size strips
½ cup shredded cheddar cheese (2 ounces)

In a Dutch oven or large saucepan cook pasta and carrots in a large amount of boiling salted water for 7 minutes, stirring occasionally. Add broccoli flowerets. Return to boiling and cook for 3 to 5 minutes more or till pasta is tender but slightly firm and vegetables are crisp-tender. Drain; keep warm.

Meanwhile, for sauce, cook mushrooms in margarine or butter till tender. Stir in flour, parsley, and basil. Add milk all at once. Cook and stir till thickened and bubbly. Add ham and cheddar cheese, stirring till cheese melts. Pour sauce over pasta and vegetables; toss to coat. Makes 4 main-dish servings.

Nutrition information per serving: 417 calories, 23 g protein, 47 g carbohydrate, 15 g fat (6 g saturated), 33 mg cholesterol, 711 mg sodium, 590 mg potassium.

CHEESY SAUSAGE AND TORTELLINI TOSS

No time to cook? Here's a quick-and-easy supper dish to serve in a pinch.

1 cup packaged dried tricolor *or* plain
    tortellini (about ½ of a 7-ounce
    package)
3 cups broccoli flowerets
8 ounces fully cooked smoked Polish
    sausage, halved lengthwise and
    thinly bias-sliced
1 tablespoon margarine *or* butter
1 tablespoon all-purpose flour
1 teaspoon caraway seed
1 cup milk
1 cup shredded process Swiss cheese
    (4 ounces)
1 tablespoon coarse-grain brown
    mustard

In a Dutch oven or large saucepan cook tortellini in a large amount of boiling salted water for 10 minutes, stirring occasionally. Add broccoli and Polish sausage. Return to boiling and cook about 5 minutes more or till pasta is tender but slightly firm and broccoli is crisp-tender, stirring occasionally. Drain; keep warm.

Meanwhile, for sauce, in a medium saucepan melt margarine or butter. Stir in flour and caraway seed. Add milk all at once. Cook and stir till thickened and bubbly. Add Swiss cheese and brown mustard, stirring till cheese melts. Pour sauce over tortellini mixture; toss to coat. Makes 4 main-dish servings.

Nutrition information per serving: 482 calories, 26 g protein, 25 g carbohydrate, 31 g fat (12 g saturated), 70 mg cholesterol, 925 mg sodium, 503 mg potassium.

BOW TIES WITH SAUSAGE AND PEPPERS

Toss garden-fresh tomatoes and peppers with Italian sausage and pasta for a dish that captures the flavors of the Mediterranean.

  6 ounces packaged dried bow ties *or* rope
      macaroni (gemelli)
 12 ounces fresh sweet *or* hot Italian
      sausage links, cut into ½-inch pieces
  1 medium onion, chopped (½ cup)
  2 cloves garlic, minced
  1 large red sweet pepper, cut into 1-inch
      pieces
  1 large green pepper, cut into 1-inch
      pieces
  1 cup sliced fresh mushrooms
  ⅔ cup chicken broth
  1 tablespoon snipped fresh basil *or*
      1 teaspoon dried basil, crushed
  2 teaspoons cornstarch
  1 large tomato, coarsely chopped (1 cup)

Cook pasta according to the directions on page 140. Drain; keep warm.

Meanwhile, in a large skillet cook the sausage, onion, and garlic for 5 minutes. Add red sweet pepper, green pepper, and mushrooms. Cook about 5 minutes more or till sausage is brown. Drain fat.

Combine broth, basil, and cornstarch. Add to sausage mixture. Cook and stir till thickened and bubbly. Cook and stir for 2 minutes more. Stir in tomato; heat through. Pour sausage mixture over pasta; toss to mix. Makes 4 main-dish servings.

Nutrition information per serving: 412 calories, 20 g protein, 43 g carbohydrate, 17 g fat (6 g saturated), 49 mg cholesterol, 712 mg sodium, 555 mg potassium.

SAUSAGE AND MOSTACCIOLI WITH RICH CREAM SAUCE

The rich cream sauce is the perfect foil for sweet and spicy Italian sausage.

8	ounces packaged dried mostaccioli *or* corkscrew macaroni
12	ounces bulk sweet Italian sausage *or* ground turkey sausage
2	cups sliced fresh shiitake mushrooms *or* sliced fresh mushrooms
1	small red sweet *or* green pepper, cut into bite-size pieces
1	medium onion, chopped (½ cup)
1	clove garlic, minced
1½	cups whipping cream
2	tablespoons snipped fresh basil *or* ½ teaspoon dried basil, crushed
¼	teaspoon pepper
½	cup grated Parmesan cheese Fresh basil leaves (optional)

Cook pasta according to the directions on page 140. Drain; keep warm.

For sauce, in a large skillet cook sausage, mushrooms, red sweet or green pepper, onion, and garlic till the sausage is brown. Drain fat.

Stir whipping cream, basil, and pepper into sausage mixture. Cook over medium-low heat for 5 to 8 minutes or till slightly thickened, stirring occasionally. Remove from heat. Stir the cheese into the sauce.

Arrange the pasta on individual plates or a large platter. Spoon the sauce over the pasta. If desired, garnish with fresh basil leaves. Makes 4 main-dish servings.

Nutrition information per serving: 802 calories, 28 g protein, 51 g carbohydrate, 54 g fat (29 g saturated), 181 mg cholesterol, 847 mg sodium, 442 mg potassium.

TRATTORIA-STYLE FETTUCCINE

This fettuccine is just the kind of pasta dish that neighborhood trattorias take pride in serving. It tosses an intensely flavored double-tomato sauce with tangy feta cheese.

1 **9-ounce package refrigerated spinach fettuccine**
2 **tablespoons chopped shallot *or* green onion**
1 **medium carrot, coarsely shredded**
1 **tablespoon olive oil**
¼ **cup oil-packed dried tomatoes, drained and snipped**
4 **medium red *and/or* yellow tomatoes, coarsely chopped (2²/₃ cups)**
½ **cup crumbled garlic and herb *or* peppercorn feta cheese (2 ounces)**

Using kitchen scissors, cut the stack of fettuccine strands in half crosswise (for easier eating.) Cook the pasta according to package directions; drain. Drain. Keep warm.

Meanwhile, in a large skillet cook shallot or green onion and carrots in hot oil over medium heat for 1 to 2 minutes or till just tender. Stir in fresh and dried tomatoes; cook 1 to 2 minutes or till heated through. Spoon tomato mixture over cooked pasta; toss gently. Sprinkle individual servings with cheese. Makes 4 main-dish servings.

Nutrition information per serving: *314 calories, 13 g protein, 42 g carbohydrate, 12 g fat (4 g saturated fat), 77 mg cholesterol, 292 mg sodium, 656 mg potassium.*

SPAGHETTI WITH TURKEY MEATBALLS

We updated everyone's favorite pasta dish by using ground turkey instead of ground beef.

1   large onion, chopped (1 cup)
1   medium green pepper, coarsely
      chopped (1 cup)
1   medium carrot, coarsely chopped
      (½ cup)
1   stalk celery, sliced (½ cup)
1   tablespoon cooking oil
4   large ripe tomatoes, peeled and
      chopped (4 cups), *or* two 16-ounce
      cans tomatoes, cut up
1   6-ounce can (⅔ cup) tomato paste
2   teaspoons dried Italian seasoning,
      crushed
½   teaspoon sugar
½   teaspoon salt
½   teaspoon garlic powder
    Turkey Meatballs
12 ounces packaged dried spaghetti *or*
      mostaccioli

For sauce, in a Dutch oven cook onion, green pepper, carrot, and celery in hot oil till tender. Stir in fresh or *undrained* canned tomatoes, tomato paste, Italian seasoning, sugar, salt, and garlic powder. Bring to boiling; add Turkey Meatballs. Reduce heat; cover and simmer for 30 minutes. If necessary, uncover and simmer for 10 to 15 minutes more or till sauce is desired consistency, stirring occasionally.

Meanwhile, cook pasta according to the directions on page 140. Drain.

Arrange pasta on individual plates or a large platter. Spoon the meatballs and sauce over pasta. Makes 6 main-dish servings.

Turkey Meatballs: In a medium mixing bowl combine 1 beaten *egg;* 2 tablespoons *milk;* ¼ cup *fine dry bread crumbs;* ½ teaspoon *salt;* ½ teaspoon dried *Italian seasoning,* crushed; and ½ teaspoon *pepper.* Add 1 pound *ground raw turkey;* mix well. With wet hands, shape turkey mixture into twenty-four 1-inch meatballs. Place the meatballs in a greased 13x9x2-inch baking pan. Bake in a 375° oven for 20 minutes or till no pink remains in meat; drain fat.

Nutrition information per serving: 442 calories, 22 g protein, 65 g carbohydrate, 11 g fat (2 g saturated), 64 mg cholesterol, 686 mg sodium, 841 mg potassium.

SPINACH FETTUCCINE WITH CHICKEN AND ARTICHOKE HEARTS

Walnuts give this dish a distinct sophistication along with a wonderful flavor.

4 skinless, boneless chicken breast halves (about 12 ounces total) *or* 12 ounces boneless beef top round steak
8 ounces packaged dried spinach *or* plain fettuccine
1 6½-ounce jar marinated artichoke hearts
1 clove garlic, minced
1 cup coarsely chopped walnuts
1 medium onion, chopped (½ cup)
1 teaspoon dried basil, crushed
½ teaspoon dried tarragon, crushed
2 tablespoons finely shredded *or* grated Parmesan cheese

Rinse chicken and pat dry. Cut into thin bite-size strips. (For beef, partially freeze beef. Trim fat from beef. Thinly slice beef across the grain into bite-size strips.) Set aside.

Cook pasta according to the directions on page 140. Drain; keep warm.

Meanwhile, drain artichoke hearts, reserving marinade. Pour 2 tablespoons reserved marinade into a wok or large skillet (add more marinade as necessary during cooking.) Heat marinade over medium-high heat. Add garlic; stir-fry for 15 seconds. Add walnuts, onion, basil, and tarragon; stir-fry about 2 minutes or till onion is crisp-tender. Remove walnut mixture from the wok.

Add the chicken or beef to the wok or skillet. Stir-fry for 2 to 3 minutes or till no pink remains in the chicken or till beef is desired doneness. Return the walnut mixture to the wok. Stir in artichoke hearts. Cook and stir for 1 minute or till heated through.

Arrange the pasta on individual plates or a large platter. Spoon the chicken mixture over the pasta. Sprinkle with Parmesan cheese. Makes 4 main-dish servings.

Nutrition information per serving: 549 calories, 30 g protein, 53 g carbohydrate, 26 g fat (3 g saturated), 47 mg cholesterol, 257 mg sodium, 509 mg potassium.

LINGUINE WITH CHICKEN AND PEANUT SAUCE

This garlic- and ginger-scented chicken dinner offers an Oriental twist.

8   ounces packaged dried linguine *or* spaghetti
1   14½-ounce can chicken broth
2   tablespoons dry white wine *or* water
2   tablespoons soy sauce
1   tablespoon cornstarch
⅛   to ¼ teaspoon ground red pepper
½   cup peanut butter
1   tablespoon cooking oil
1   medium onion, halved lengthwise and thinly sliced
2   cloves garlic, minced
1   teaspoon grated gingerroot
4   medium skinless, boneless chicken breast halves (about 12 ounces), cut into 1-inch pieces
2   green onions, sliced (¼ cup)
    Orange slices, cut in half (optional)
    Grapes (optional)

Cook pasta according to the directions on page 140. Drain; keep warm.

For sauce, in a medium mixing bowl stir together chicken broth, wine or water, soy sauce, cornstarch, and red pepper. Stir in peanut butter till smooth. Set sauce aside.

In a wok or large skillet heat the cooking oil over medium-high heat. (Add more oil as necessary during cooking.) Add onion, garlic, and gingerroot to hot oil; stir-fry for 2 to 3 minutes or till onion is crisp-tender. Remove onion mixture from skillet.

Add the chicken to the wok. Stir-fry about 3 minutes or till chicken is no longer pink. Push the chicken from the center of the wok. Stir sauce; add to center of the wok. Cook and stir till thickened and bubbly. Cook and stir for 2 minutes more. Return onion mixture to the skillet; stir all the ingredients together.

Arrange pasta on individual plates or a large platter. Spoon the chicken mixture over pasta. Sprinkle with green onions. If desired, garnish with orange slices and grapes. Makes 4 main-dish servings.

Nutrition information per serving: 579 calories, 35 g protein, 57 g carbohydrate, 23 g fat (5 g saturated), 45 mg cholesterol, 1,038 mg sodium, 566 mg potassium.

PASTA WITH CHICKEN AND PEPPER-CHEESE SAUCE

Ground red, white, and black peppers multiply the hotness by three in this zippy cream sauce.

8 ounces packaged dried spaghetti *or* fettuccine
1 tablespoon all-purpose flour
½ teaspoon salt
¼ to ½ teaspoon ground red pepper
⅛ to ¼ teaspoon ground white pepper
⅛ to ¼ teaspoon ground black pepper
3 small skinless, boneless chicken breast halves (about 8 ounces total), cut into 1-inch pieces
1 tablespoon cooking oil
1 medium red sweet *or* green pepper, chopped (1 cup)
1 medium onion, chopped (½ cup)
1 tablespoon chopped, seeded jalapeño pepper
2 cloves garlic, minced
2 tablespoons all-purpose flour
¾ cup chicken broth
½ cup milk
1 teaspoon Worcestershire sauce
1 cup shredded Monterey Jack *or* cheddar cheese (4 ounces)
¼ cup dairy sour cream
1 jalapeño pepper, thinly sliced (optional)

Cook pasta according to the directions on page 140. Drain; keep warm.

In a small mixing bowl combine 1 tablespoon flour, salt, red pepper, white pepper, and black pepper. Toss flour mixture with chicken to coat. Set aside.

In a large skillet heat the cooking oil over medium-high heat. (Add more oil as necessary during cooking.) Add red sweet or green pepper, onion, chopped jalapeño pepper, and garlic; cook and stir till the vegetables are tender. Remove vegetables with a slotted spoon; set aside.

Add chicken to the skillet. Cook and stir for 4 to 5 minutes or till chicken is no longer pink. Remove chicken from skillet.

Stir 2 tablespoons flour into drippings in skillet. Add chicken broth, milk, and Worcestershire sauce. Cook and stir till thickened and bubbly. Add the Monterey Jack or cheddar cheese, stirring till cheese melts. Stir *1 cup* of the hot mixture into the sour cream; return all of the sour cream mixture to skillet. Stir in chicken and vegetables. Cook till heated through. *Do not boil.*

Arrange pasta on individual plates or a large platter. Spoon the chicken mixture over pasta. If desired, garnish with jalapeño pepper slices. Makes 4 main-dish servings.

Nutrition information per serving: 512 calories, 29 g protein, 56 g carbohydrate, 19 g fat (9 g saturated), 64 mg cholesterol, 660 mg sodium, 355 mg potassium.

LINGUINE WITH SMOKED SALMON IN CREAM SAUCE

If you are using the smoked salmon, omit the salt when cooking the pasta. You'll find the smoked salmon adds all the saltiness you need.

8   ounces packaged dried linguine, fettuccine, *or* spaghetti
6   ounces thinly sliced, smoked salmon (lox-style) *or* cooked fresh salmon
2   green onions, thinly sliced (¼ cup)
1   clove garlic, minced
1   tablespoon margarine *or* butter
1   cup whipping cream
1   tablespoon snipped fresh dill *or* 1 teaspoon dried dillweed
1   teaspoon finely shredded lemon peel
¼   teaspoon pepper
2   tablespoons grated Parmesan cheese
     Fresh dill sprigs (optional)

Cook pasta according to the directions on page 140. Drain; keep warm.

Meanwhile, cut the salmon into thin bite-size strips; set aside.

For sauce, in a large skillet cook the green onion and garlic in margarine or butter till tender. Add salmon and cook for 1 minute. Stir in whipping cream, 1 tablespoon fresh dill or 1 teaspoon dried dillweed, lemon peel, and pepper. Bring to boiling; reduce heat. Cook at a gentle boil about 5 minutes or till the sauce thickens slightly. Remove from heat. Stir in Parmesan cheese.

Arrange the pasta on individual plates or a large platter. Spoon the sauce over the pasta. If desired, garnish with fresh dill sprigs. Makes 4 main-dish servings.

Nutrition information per serving: 523 calories, 18 g protein, 48 g carbohydrate, 29 g fat (15 g saturated), 94 mg cholesterol, 450 mg sodium, 194 mg potassium.

LINGUINE WITH CLAMS AND DRIED TOMATOES

Dried tomatoes give a robust flavor to this classic pasta dish. Look for them in specialty shops or the gourmet section of your grocery store.

8 ounces packaged dried linguine,
     fettuccine, *or* spaghetti
2 6½-ounce cans chopped *or*
     minced clams
1 medium onion, chopped (½ cup)
2 cloves garlic, minced
¼ teaspoon crushed red pepper
2 tablespoons olive oil *or* cooking oil
½ cup dry white wine
⅓ cup oil-packed dried tomatoes, drained
     and cut into strips
2 tablespoons snipped parsley
     Parsley sprigs (optional)

Cook pasta according to the directions on page 140. Drain; keep warm.

Meanwhile, for sauce, drain clams, reserving liquid. In a medium saucepan cook onion, garlic, and crushed red pepper in hot oil. Stir in reserved clam liquid and wine. Bring to boiling. Boil gently about 10 minutes or till sauce is reduced to about 1 cup. Stir in clams, tomatoes, and the 2 tablespoons parsley; heat through.

Arrange the pasta on individual plates or a large platter. Spoon the sauce over the pasta. If desired, garnish with parsley sprigs. Makes 4 main-dish servings.

Nutrition information per serving: 387 calories, 16 g protein, 53 g carbohydrate, 11 g fat (2 g saturated), 57 mg cholesterol, 58 mg sodium, 312 mg potassium.

ORANGE SHRIMP WITH FETTUCCINE

Peel and section the oranges over a bowl to catch the juices.

12 ounces fresh *or* frozen, peeled, deveined
 shrimp
6 ounces packaged dried fettuccine *or*
 linguine
1 red sweet *or* green pepper, cut into
 ¾-inch squares
1 tablespoon cooking oil
½ teaspoon finely shredded orange peel
⅔ cup orange juice
1 tablespoon cornstarch
1 teaspoon instant chicken bouillon
 granules
½ teaspoon toasted sesame oil
¼ teaspoon salt
⅛ teaspoon ground red pepper
1 6-ounce package frozen pea pods,
 thawed
2 oranges, peeled and sectioned

Thaw shrimp, if frozen.

Cook pasta according to the directions on page 140. Drain; keep warm.

Meanwhile, in a large skillet cook the red sweet or green pepper squares in hot oil for 1 to 2 minutes or till crisp-tender. Remove pepper squares. Add shrimp; cook and stir about 2 minutes more or till shrimp turn pink. Remove shrimp.

Combine orange peel, orange juice, cornstarch, bouillon granules, sesame oil, salt, and ground red pepper. Add to skillet. Cook and stir till thickened and bubbly. Return shrimp and peppers to the skillet; stir till coated. Gently stir in pea pods and orange sections. Heat through.

Arrange pasta on individual plates or a large platter. Spoon the shrimp mixture over pasta. Makes 4 main-dish servings.

Nutrition information per serving: 337 calories, 22 g protein, 49 g carbohydrate, 6 g fat (1 g saturated), 131 mg cholesterol, 503 mg sodium, 417 mg potassium.

FETTUCCINE WITH HERBED SHRIMP

A white wine and herb sauce dresses the shrimp and pasta in this elegant entree.

12 ounces fresh *or* frozen, peeled, deveined shrimp
6 ounces packaged dried plain *and/or* spinach fettuccine
2 cups sliced fresh mushrooms
1 large onion, chopped (1 cup)
2 cloves garlic, minced
1 tablespoon olive oil *or* cooking oil
¼ cup dry white wine
1 tablespoon instant chicken bouillon granules
1 tablespoon snipped fresh basil *or* 1 teaspoon dried basil, crushed
1½ teaspoons snipped fresh oregano *or* ½ teaspoon dried oregano, crushed
1 teaspoon cornstarch
⅛ teaspoon pepper
2 medium tomatoes, peeled, seeded, and chopped
¼ cup grated Parmesan cheese
¼ cup snipped parsley

Thaw shrimp, if frozen. Cut shrimp in half lengthwise; set aside.

Cook pasta according to the directions on page 140. Drain; keep warm.

Meanwhile, in a large saucepan cook mushrooms, onion, and garlic in hot oil till onion is tender but not brown.

In a small mixing bowl stir together wine, bouillon granules, basil, oregano, cornstarch, and pepper. Add to saucepan. Cook and stir till thickened and bubbly.

Add shrimp to wine mixture. Cover and simmer about 2 minutes or till shrimp turn pink. Stir in tomatoes; heat through.

Spoon the shrimp mixture over pasta. Sprinkle with Parmesan cheese and parsley. Toss to mix. Makes 4 main-dish servings.

Nutrition information per serving: 351 calories, 25 g protein, 44 g carbohydrate, 7 g fat (2 g saturated), 136 mg cholesterol, 926 mg sodium, 549 mg potassium.

FETTUCCINE AND SCALLOPS WITH WINE SAUCE

Plan a special occasion repast around this black-tie pasta dish.

1 pound fresh *or* frozen scallops
6 ounces packaged dried plain *and/or*
       spinach fettuccine *or* linguine
3 cups sliced fresh mushrooms
4 medium carrots, thinly sliced (2 cups)
8 green onions, sliced (1 cup)
½ cup dry white wine
1 tablespoon cornstarch
½ teaspoon instant chicken bouillon
       granules
2 tablespoons margarine *or* butter
3 to 4 cloves garlic, minced
2 tablespoons snipped parsley
½ teaspoon lemon-pepper seasoning

Thaw scallops, if frozen. Cut any large scallops in half.

In a 4½-quart Dutch oven bring 3 quarts *water* to boiling. Add pasta; return to boiling. Cook for 5 minutes. Add mushrooms, carrots, and green onions. Return to boiling. Cook, uncovered, for 5 to 7 minutes more or till pasta is tender but slightly firm and vegetables are crisp-tender. Drain pasta and vegetables; keep warm.

Meanwhile, in a small mixing bowl stir together wine, cornstarch, and bouillon granules; set aside.

In a large skillet melt margarine or butter. Add garlic; cook over medium-high heat about 1 minute. Add scallops, wine mixture, parsley, and lemon-pepper seasoning to skillet. Cook and stir over medium heat till thickened and bubbly. Cook and stir for 1 to 2 minutes more or till scallops turn opaque.

Arrange pasta mixture on individual plates or a large platter. Spoon the scallop mixture over pasta mixture. Makes 4 main-dish servings.

Nutrition information per serving: 364 calories, 23 g protein, 47 g carbohydrate, 8 g fat (1 g saturated), 34 mg cholesterol, 505 mg sodium, 788 mg potassium.

PASTA PRIMAVERA

A great dish to celebrate summertime and garden-fresh vegetables.

8 ounces fresh wax *or* green beans, cut into 2-inch pieces (2 cups)
8 ounces fresh asparagus, cut into 2-inch pieces (1½ cups)
1 cup broccoli flowerets
8 ounces packaged dried vermicelli *or* spaghetti
½ of a medium red sweet *or* green pepper, cut into 1-inch pieces
2 green onions, sliced (¼ cup)
1 tablespoon margarine *or* butter
1¼ cups chicken broth
    Dash ground nutmeg
1 8-ounce carton plain low-fat yogurt
3 tablespoons all-purpose flour
½ cup grated Parmesan cheese
½ cup pine nuts *or* slivered almonds, toasted

In a large saucepan cook wax or green beans in a small amount of boiling salted water for 15 minutes. Add asparagus and broccoli. Cook for 5 to 10 minutes more or till vegetables are crisp-tender. Drain; keep warm while preparing sauce.

Meanwhile, cook pasta according to the directions on page 140. Drain; keep warm while preparing sauce.

For sauce, in a medium saucepan cook red sweet or green pepper and green onions in margarine or butter till tender but not brown. Stir in chicken broth and nutmeg. Bring to boiling; reduce heat. Stir together yogurt and flour. Add yogurt mixture to saucepan. Cook and stir till thickened and bubbly. Stir in Parmesan cheese. Cook and stir for 1 minute more or till the sauce is smooth. Pour sauce over cooked vegetables; toss gently to coat.

Arrange the pasta on individual plates or a large platter. Spoon the sauce over the pasta. Sprinkle with pine nuts or slivered almonds. Makes 4 main-dish servings.

Nutrition information per serving: 510 calories, 25 g protein, 64 g carbohydrate, 20 g fat (5 g saturated), 13 mg cholesterol, 557 mg sodium, 699 mg potassium.

PASTA TWISTS WITH BEER-CHEESE SAUCE

Be sure to use sharp cheddar for the cheesiest flavor.

8 ounces packaged dried tri-colored
    corkscrew macaroni *or* rope
    macaroni (gemelli)
2 medium carrots, bias-sliced (1 cup)
1 small zucchini, coarsely chopped
    (1 cup)
1 cup fresh whole mushrooms, quartered
2 tablespoons margarine *or* butter
2 tablespoons all-purpose flour
1 cup milk
¼ cup beer
¾ cup shredded sharp cheddar cheese
    (3 ounces)

Cook pasta according to the directions on page 140. Drain; keep warm.

Meanwhile, for sauce, in a medium saucepan cook carrots, zucchini, and mushrooms in margarine or butter till vegetables are tender. Stir in flour. Add milk all at once. Cook and stir over medium heat till thickened and bubbly. Cook and stir for 1 minute more. Add beer and heat through. Remove pan from heat. Gradually add cheddar cheese, stirring just till melted. If desired, season to taste with salt and pepper.

Arrange pasta on individual plates or a large platter. Spoon the sauce over pasta. Makes 4 main-dish servings.

Nutrition information per serving: 426 calories, 16 g protein, 55 g carbohydrate, 15 g fat (6 g saturated), 27 mg cholesterol, 253 mg sodium, 381 mg potassium.

BAKED MOSTACCIOLI WITH MEAT SAUCE

Bake these single-serving casseroles, topped with lots of melted cheese, for a hot and satisfying supper.

8   ounces packaged dried mostaccioli *or* cavatelli
1   16-ounce can plum tomatoes
½   of a 6-ounce can (⅓ cup) tomato paste
¼   cup dry red wine *or* water
½   teaspoon sugar
½   teaspoon dried oregano, crushed
½   teaspoon dried thyme, crushed
¼   teaspoon pepper
1   pound ground beef
1   medium onion, chopped (½ cup)
1   clove garlic, minced
½   cup sliced pimiento-stuffed green olives
1   cup shredded mozzarella cheese
     (4 ounces)

Cook pasta according to the directions on page 140. Drain pasta; rinse with cold water. Drain again.

In a blender container or food processor bowl combine *undrained* tomatoes, tomato paste, wine or water, sugar, oregano, thyme, and pepper. Cover and blend or process till smooth. Set aside.

In a large skillet cook ground beef, onion, and garlic till meat is brown. Drain fat. Stir in tomato mixture. Bring to boiling; reduce heat. Cover and simmer for 10 minutes. Stir in pasta and olives.

Divide the pasta mixture among six 10-ounce casseroles. Bake in a 375° oven for 15 minutes. (*Or,* spoon all of the pasta mixture into a 2-quart casserole and bake for 30 minutes.) Sprinkle with mozzarella cheese. Bake 5 minutes more or till heated through. Makes 6 main-dish servings.

Nutrition information per serving: 367 calories, 25 g protein, 38 g carbohydrate, 13 g fat (5 g saturated), 58 mg cholesterol, 572 mg sodium, 521 mg potassium.

PASTA PIZZA

This hybrid recipe arranges favorite casserole ingredients to create an outstanding dish that looks and tastes like pizza.

5   ounces packaged dried corkscrew
      macaroni (2 cups)
1   beaten egg
¼   cup milk
2   tablespoons grated Parmesan cheese
8   ounces ground beef
1   small onion, chopped (⅓ cup)
1   clove garlic, minced
1   medium green *and/or* yellow
      sweet pepper, cut into 2-inch strips
1   14½-ounce can Italian-style stewed
      tomatoes
½   teaspoon dried Italian seasoning,
      crushed
1   4½-ounce jar sliced mushrooms,
      drained
¼   teaspoon crushed red pepper
1   cup shredded mozzarella cheese
      (4 ounces)

Cook pasta according to the directions on page 140. Drain pasta; rinse with cold water. Drain again.

For pasta crust, in a large mixing bowl combine egg, milk, and Parmesan cheese. Stir in pasta. Spread pasta mixture evenly in a greased 12-inch pizza pan. Bake in a 350° oven for 20 minutes.

Meanwhile, in a large skillet cook ground beef, onion, and garlic till meat is brown. Drain fat. Add pepper strips, *undrained* tomatoes (cut up any large pieces of tomato), and Italian seasoning to meat mixture. Bring to boiling; reduce heat. Simmer, uncovered, for 10 to 12 minutes or till peppers are crisp-tender and most of the liquid is evaporated, stirring once or twice. Stir in mushrooms and crushed red pepper.

Spoon meat mixture over pasta crust. Sprinkle with mozzarella cheese. Bake for 10 to 12 minutes more or till heated through and cheese is melted. To serve, cut into wedges. Makes 6 main-dish servings.

Nutrition information per serving: 259 calories, 18 g protein, 27 g carbohydrate, 9 g fat (4 g saturated), 72 mg cholesterol, 479 mg sodium, 393 mg potassium.

STUFFED MANICOTTI WITH PEPPERY CHEESE SAUCE

Walnuts make a surprise appearance in the beefy filling.

12	packaged dried manicotti shells
1	medium onion, chopped (½ cup)
1	clove garlic, minced
3	tablespoons margarine *or* butter
3	tablespoons all-purpose flour
1½	teaspoons instant chicken bouillon granules
½	teaspoon paprika
¼	to ½ teaspoon ground red pepper
¼	to ½ teaspoon ground black pepper
2¼	cups milk
1	cup shredded process Swiss cheese (4 ounces)
12	ounces ground beef *or* pork
1	cup frozen peas
¾	cup chopped walnuts
2	tablespoons diced pimiento
	Sliced green onion (optional)
	Diced pimiento (optional)

Cook the manicotti shells according to the directions on page 140. Drain shells; rinse with cold water. Drain again.

For sauce, in a medium saucepan cook the onion and garlic in the margarine or butter till onion is tender. Stir in flour, bouillon granules, paprika, red pepper, and black pepper. Add milk all at once. Cook and stir till thickened and bubbly. Cook and stir for 1 minute more. Gradually add cheese, stirring till melted. Remove from heat.

In a large skillet cook the ground beef or pork till brown. Drain fat. Stir in peas, walnuts, 2 tablespoons pimiento, and *1 cup* of the sauce. Fill *each* manicotti with about ¼ *cup* of the meat mixture. Arrange manicotti in six individual au gratin dishes or in a 3-quart rectangular baking dish. Pour the remaining sauce over the filled manicotti. Cover manicotti with foil.

Bake in a 350° oven about 20 minutes for individual dishes or about 35 minutes for the baking dish or till heated through. If desired, sprinkle with sliced green onion and additional diced pimiento. Makes 6 main-dish servings.

Nutrition information per serving: 515 calories, 26 g protein, 40 g carbohydrate, 28 g fat (8 g saturated), 58 mg cholesterol, 634 mg sodium, 502 mg potassium.

TACO SPAGHETTI

Feel like Mexican cuisine tonight? This combination of pasta, salsa, ground beef, and cheese captures south-of-the-border flavors.

5 ounces packaged dried spaghetti, linguine, *or* fettuccine, broken
1 pound ground beef *or* ground raw turkey
1 large onion, chopped (1 cup)
¾ cup water
½ of a 1¼-ounce envelope (2 tablespoons) taco seasoning mix
1 11-ounce can whole kernel corn with sweet peppers, drained
1 cup sliced pitted ripe olives
1 cup shredded Cojack *or* cheddar cheese (4 ounces)
½ cup salsa
1 4-ounce can diced green chili peppers, drained
6 cups shredded lettuce
1 cup broken tortilla chips
1 medium tomato, cut into thin wedges
   Dairy sour cream (optional)

Cook pasta according to the directions on page 140. Drain pasta; rinse with cold water. Drain again.

In a 12-inch skillet cook ground beef or turkey and onion till meat is brown. Drain fat. Stir in water and taco seasoning. Bring to boiling; reduce heat. Simmer, uncovered, for 2 minutes, stirring occasionally. Stir in cooked pasta, corn, olives, *half* of the shredded cheese, salsa, and chili peppers.

Transfer mixture to a lightly greased 2-quart round casserole. Cover and bake in a 350° oven for 15 to 20 minutes or till heated through. Sprinkle with remaining cheese.

Serve with shredded lettuce, tortilla chips, and tomato wedges. If desired, top with sour cream. Makes 6 main-dish servings.

Nutrition information per serving: 438 calories, 26 g protein, 42 g carbohydrate, 21 g fat (8 g saturated), 66 mg cholesterol, 949 mg sodium, 525 mg potassium.

SAUCY SPICED SHELLS

Eat up! A trio of these jumbo shells filled with spiced beef makes a generous serving.

12 jumbo shell macaroni
12 ounces ground beef, pork, *or* lamb
 1 medium onion, chopped (½ cup)
 ½ cup chopped green pepper
 1 clove garlic, minced
 1 beaten egg
 ¼ cup fine dry bread crumbs
 ¼ teaspoon ground cinnamon
 ¼ teaspoon ground allspice
 ¼ teaspoon pepper
 1 15-ounce container fresh refrigerated
      marinara sauce *or* plum tomato
      sauce with basil *or* one 15½-ounce
      jar meatless spaghetti sauce
    Finely shredded *or* grated Parmesan
      cheese (optional)

Cook pasta according to the directions on page 140. Drain pasta; rinse with cold water. Drain again.

In a large skillet cook ground meat, onion, green pepper, and garlic till meat is brown. Drain fat.

In a medium mixing bowl combine egg, bread crumbs, cinnamon, allspice, and pepper. Add the meat mixture and ¼ *cup* of the sauce; mix well. Spoon about *2 tablespoons* of the meat mixture into *each* macaroni shell. Arrange the filled shells in a 2-quart square baking dish. Pour the remaining sauce over the filled shells. Cover the dish with foil.

Bake in a 375° oven for 25 to 30 minutes or till heated through. For each serving, arrange *3* of the shells on individual plates. Spoon some of the sauce over the shells. If desired, sprinkle each serving with Parmesan cheese. Makes 4 main-dish servings.

Nutrition information per serving: 325 calories, 23 g protein, 30 g carbohydrate, 12 g fat (4 g saturated), 107 mg cholesterol, 445 mg sodium, 248 mg potassium.

SPAGHETTI AND SAUSAGE PIE

Good recipes never go away. Year after year, this perennial favorite keeps popping up in our test kitchen.

5   ounces packaged dried spaghetti
1   beaten egg
⅓   cup grated Parmesan cheese
1   tablespoon margarine *or* butter, cut up
1   beaten egg
1   cup cream-style cottage cheese, drained
⅛   teaspoon pepper
8   ounces bulk pork sausage, Italian
      sausage, *or* ground turkey sausage
1   cup sliced fresh mushrooms
1   medium onion, chopped (½ cup)
¼   cup chopped green pepper
1   8-ounce can pizza sauce
½   cup shredded mozzarella cheese
      (2 ounces)

Cook spaghetti according to the directions on page 140. Drain spaghetti; rinse with cold water. Drain again.

For spaghetti crust, in a medium mixing bowl combine 1 egg, Parmesan cheese, and margarine or butter. Add spaghetti; toss to coat. Press the spaghetti mixture against the bottom and sides of a well-greased 9-inch pie plate to form an even crust.

In a small mixing bowl combine 1 egg, cottage cheese, and pepper. Spread over the spaghetti crust; set aside.

In a large skillet cook the sausage, mushrooms, onion, and green pepper till the meat is brown and vegetables are tender. Drain fat. Stir in pizza sauce. Cook till heated through. Spoon meat mixture over cottage cheese mixture. Cover loosely with foil.

Bake in a 350° oven for 20 minutes. Remove foil; sprinkle with mozzarella cheese. Bake, uncovered, about 5 minutes more or till mozzarella cheese melts. Let stand 5 minutes before serving. Cut into wedges to serve. Makes 4 or 5 main-dish servings.

Nutrition information per serving: 442 calories, 30 g protein, 39 g carbohydrate, 18 g fat (6 g saturated), 155 mg cholesterol, 848 mg sodium, 552 mg potassium.

CHICKEN MANICOTTI WITH CHIVE CREAM SAUCE

Broccoli and pimiento add vivid colors to the tasty chicken filling that spills from these pasta shells.

12 packaged dried manicotti shells
1   8-ounce container soft-style cream
      cheese with chives and onion
⅔ cup milk
¼ cup grated Romano *or* Parmesan cheese
2   cups chopped cooked chicken
      (10 ounces)
1   10-ounce package frozen chopped
      broccoli, thawed and drained
½ of a 7-ounce jar roasted red
      sweet peppers, drained and sliced,
      or one 4-ounce jar diced pimiento,
      drained
¼ teaspoon pepper
    Paprika

Cook the manicotti shells according to the directions on page 140. Drain shells; rinse with cold water. Drain again.

Meanwhile, for sauce, in a small heavy saucepan melt cream cheese over medium-low heat, stirring constantly. Slowly add milk, stirring till smooth. Stir in Romano or Parmesan cheese. Remove from heat.

For filling, in a medium mixing bowl stir together ¾ *cup* of the sauce, chicken, broccoli, roasted red sweet pepper or pimiento, and pepper. Using a small spoon, carefully fill *each* manicotti shell with about ⅓ *cup* of the filling.

Arrange the filled shells in a 3-quart rectangular baking dish. Pour the remaining sauce over the shells. Sprinkle with paprika. Cover with foil.

Bake in a 350° oven for 25 to 30 minutes or till heated through. Makes 6 main-dish servings.

Nutrition information per serving: 396 calories, 25 g protein, 31 g carbohydrate, 18 g fat (9 g saturated), 92 mg cholesterol, 257 mg sodium, 389 mg potassium.

TURKEY LASAGNA ROLLS

For this robust lasagna-style entree, roll the noodles around a cheesy spinach filling and then top them with a turkey and tomato sauce.

8 ounces ground raw turkey
1 medium onion, chopped (½ cup)
2 cloves garlic, minced
1 cup sliced fresh mushrooms
1 cup water
1 7½-ounce can (⅞ cup) tomatoes, cut up
1 6-ounce can tomato paste
1½ teaspoons dried oregano, crushed
1 teaspoon dried basil, crushed
8 packaged dried lasagna noodles
1 beaten egg
1 15-ounce carton ricotta cheese
1 10-ounce package frozen chopped spinach, thawed and drained
1½ cups shredded mozzarella cheese (6 ounces)
1 cup grated Parmesan cheese
Fresh parsley sprigs (optional)

For sauce, in a large skillet cook turkey, onion, and garlic till turkey is no longer pink; drain fat. Stir in mushrooms, water, *undrained* tomatoes, tomato paste, oregano, and basil. Bring to boiling; reduce heat. Cover and simmer for 25 minutes.

Meanwhile, cook lasagna noodles according to the directions on page 140. Drain noodles; rinse with cold water. Drain again.

For filling, in a mixing bowl stir together egg, ricotta cheese, spinach, *1 cup* of the mozzarella cheese, and ¾ *cup* of the Parmesan cheese.

Spread about ½ *cup* of the filling on *each* lasagna noodle. Starting from a narrow end, roll up *each* lasagna noodle. Place lasagna rolls in a 2-quart rectangular baking dish. Pour sauce over lasagna rolls. Cover dish with foil.

Bake in a 375° oven for 25 minutes. Remove foil. Sprinkle with remaining mozzarella cheese. Bake for 5 to 10 minutes more or till heated through. Let stand 5 minutes before serving. Sprinkle with remaining Parmesan cheese and, if desired, garnish with parsley sprigs. Makes 8 main-dish servings.

Nutrition information per serving: 345 calories, 26 g protein, 28 g carbohydrate, 15 g fat (8 g saturated), 75 mg cholesterol, 511 mg sodium, 616 mg potassium.

PASTITSIO

For a leaner version of this classic Greek casserole, try the ground turkey option.

4 ounces packaged dried cut ziti (1⅓ cups) *or* elbow macaroni (1 cup)
1 pound ground raw turkey, lamb, *or* beef
1 medium onion, chopped (½ cup)
2 cloves garlic, minced
1 8-ounce can tomato sauce
¼ cup dry red wine *or* beef broth
2 tablespoons snipped parsley
½ teaspoon dried oregano, crushed
¼ teaspoon salt
¼ teaspoon ground cinnamon
½ cup grated Parmesan cheese
3 tablespoons margarine *or* butter
3 tablespoons all-purpose flour
¼ teaspoon pepper
1½ cups milk
1 egg, beaten
¼ cup Parmesan cheese
Ground cinnamon (optional)

Cook pasta according to the directions on page 140. Drain pasta; rinse with cold water. Drain again.

Meanwhile, in a large skillet cook turkey, lamb, or beef; onion; and garlic till meat is brown and onion is tender. Drain fat. Stir in tomato sauce, wine or beef broth, parsley, oregano, salt, and cinnamon. Bring to boiling; reduce heat. Simmer, uncovered, for 5 minutes. Remove from heat. Stir in ½ cup Parmesan cheese.

For sauce, in a medium saucepan melt margarine or butter. Stir in flour and pepper. Add the milk all at once. Cook and stir till thickened and bubbly. Stir about *half* of the mixture into the beaten egg. Return egg mixture to the saucepan. Cook and stir for 2 minutes more. Stir in ¼ cup Parmesan cheese.

To assemble, in a 2-quart square baking dish layer *half* of the pasta, *all* of the meat mixture, remaining pasta, and *all* of the sauce. If desired, sprinkle with addititional cinnamon.

Bake in a 350° oven for 30 to 35 minutes or till set. Let stand 5 minutes before serving. Makes 6 main-dish servings.

Nutrition information per serving: 356 calories, 22 g protein, 26 g carbohydrate, 18 g fat (6 saturated), 78 mg cholesterol, 694 mg sodium, 436 mg potassium.

CHEESY CHICKEN AND MOSTACCIOLI

Monterey Jack cheese with jalapeño peppers gives a Tex-Mex accent to this creamy chicken and pasta dish.

6 ounces packaged dried mostaccioli with tomato, red pepper, and basil *or* plain mostaccioli

2 cups loose-pack frozen mixed vegetables

1 medium onion, chopped (½ cup)

2 tablespoons margarine *or* butter

2 tablespoons all-purpose flour

2 teaspoons instant chicken bouillon granules

2 cups milk

1½ cups shredded Monterey Jack cheese with jalapeño peppers (6 ounces)

2 tablespoons snipped cilantro *or* parsley

1½ cups chopped cooked chicken (about 8 ounces) *or* one 9¼-ounce can tuna, drained and broken into chunks

1 medium tomato, halved and sliced

In a large saucepan or Dutch oven bring about 3 quarts water to boiling. Add pasta. Return to boiling; cook for 9 minutes. Add frozen mixed vegetables. Return to boiling; cook for 5 to 7 minutes more or till pasta is tender but slightly firm and vegetables are crisp-tender. Drain; rinse with cold water. Drain again.

For sauce, in a large saucepan cook onion in margarine or butter till tender. Stir in flour and bouillon granules. Add milk all at once. Cook and stir till thickened and bubbly. Add cheese, stirring till melted. Stir in cilantro or parsley. Remove from heat.

Add pasta and chicken or tuna to the sauce; toss to coat. Spoon mixture into a 2-quart square baking dish. Cover dish with foil.

Bake in a 375° oven for 20 minutes. Remove foil from dish. Arrange tomato slice halves on top of pasta mixture. Bake, uncovered, for 5 to 10 minutes more or till heated through. Let stand 10 minutes before serving. Makes 6 main-dish servings.

Nutrition information per serving: 417 calories, 27 g protein, 38 g carbohydrate, 18 g fat (8 g saturated), 65 mg cholesterol, 582 mg sodium, 445 mg potassium.

SWISS CHICKEN BUNDLES

This tarragon-scented lasagna makes an elegant dish for a bridal or baby shower.

8   packaged dried lasagna noodles
1   beaten egg
2   cups ricotta cheese *or* cream-style
     cottage cheese, drained
1½   cups chopped cooked chicken
     (8 ounces)
1½   teaspoons snipped fresh tarragon *or*
     basil *or* ¼ teaspoon dried tarragon
     or basil, crushed
2   tablespoons margarine *or* butter
2   tablespoons all-purpose flour
½   teaspoon dry mustard
¼   teaspoon salt
⅛   teaspoon pepper
1½   cups milk
1½   cups shredded process Swiss cheese
     (6 ounces)
     Paprika *or* snipped parsley (optional)
     Fresh tarragon sprigs (optional)

Cook lasagna noodles according to the directions on page 140. Drain noodles; rinse with cold water. Drain again.

For filling, in a medium mixing bowl stir together egg, ricotta or cottage cheese, chicken, and 1½ teaspoons tarragon or basil.

To assemble bundles, spread about ⅓ *cup* of the filling over each lasagna noodle. Roll up noodles, starting from a short end. Place bundles, seam-side down, in a 2-quart rectangular baking dish; set aside.

For sauce, in a medium saucepan melt the margarine or butter. Stir in flour, mustard, salt, and pepper. Add milk all at once. Cook and stir till thickened and bubbly. Gradually add cheese, stirring till melted after each addition. Pour sauce over lasagna bundles. Cover dish with foil.

Bake in a 375° oven for 30 to 35 minutes or till heated through. Let stand 10 minutes before serving. Transfer bundles to individual plates. Stir sauce in baking dish. Spoon some of the sauce over *each* bundle and, if desired, sprinkle with paprika or parsley. If desired, garnish with fresh tarragon sprigs. Makes 8 main-dish servings.

Nutrition information per serving: 347 calories, 25 g protein, 22 g carbohydrate, 17 g fat (8 g saturated), 92 mg cholesterol, 523 mg sodium, 291 mg potassium.

DEVILED FISH AND PASTA

Lean fish and low-fat yogurt make this a delicious choice for those who want to lighten up their meals.

12 ounces fresh *or* frozen cod, orange roughy, *or* flounder fillets
1½ cups dry white wine *or* chicken broth
1 cup packaged dried small shell macaroni
1 8-ounce carton plain low-fat yogurt
1 stalk celery, thinly sliced (½ cup)
1 tablespoon Worcestershire sauce
2 teaspoons Dijon-style mustard
¼ teaspoon salt
   Dash ground red pepper
¼ cup grated Parmesan *or* Romano cheese
2 tablespoons fine dry bread crumbs
1 tablespoon snipped chives
1 tablespoon margarine *or* butter, melted
   Paprika
   Fresh chives (optional)

Thaw fish, if frozen. Measure thickness of fish fillets.

In a large skillet bring wine or broth to boiling. Add fish. Return to boiling; reduce heat. Cover and simmer till fish just begins to flake (allow 4 to 6 minutes per ½-inch thickness of fish). Drain fish; discarding liquid. Cut fish into bite-size pieces.

Meanwhile, cook pasta according to the directions on page 140. Drain pasta; rinse with cold water. Drain again.

In a large mixing bowl stir together yogurt, celery, Worcestershire sauce, mustard, salt, and red pepper. Add fish and pasta. Toss gently to coat. Spoon pasta mixture into four au gratin dishes.

Toss together Parmesan or Romano cheese, bread crumbs, 1 tablespoon chives, and margarine or butter. Sprinkle crumb mixture over pasta mixture. Sprinkle crumb mixture with paprika.

Bake in a 400° oven about 15 minutes or till heated through and crumbs are golden. If desired, garnish with additional chives. Makes 4 main-dish servings.

Nutrition information per serving: 344 calories, 24 g protein, 30 g carbohydrate, 7 g fat (3 g saturated), 42 mg cholesterol, 507 mg sodium, 456 mg potassium.

CREAMY SEAFOOD LASAGNA

Tender morsels of seafood in a sour cream sauce takes lasagna to new heights.

1½ cups dry white wine *or* water
1   12-ounce package frozen fish fillets
1   8-ounce package frozen, peeled,
      deveined shrimp
6   packaged dried lasagna noodles
1   beaten egg
2   cups ricotta cheese *or* cream-style
      cottage cheese, drained
½   cup grated Parmesan cheese
4   teaspoons snipped fresh basil *or*
      1 teaspoon dried basil, crushed
1   cup sliced fresh mushrooms
2   green onions, sliced (¼ cup)
3   tablespoons margarine *or* butter
3   tablespoons all-purpose flour
¼   teaspoon salt
¼   teaspoon ground white pepper
1⅓ cups milk
½   cup dairy sour cream
1   8-ounce package sliced mozzarella
      cheese
     Fresh basil leaves (optional)

In a large skillet bring wine or water to boiling. Add frozen fish fillets; cook for 4 minutes. Add shrimp; cook for 2 to 3 minutes more or till fish flakes with a fork and shrimp turn pink. Drain; discarding cooking liquid. Cut fish into bite-size pieces. Coarsely chop shrimp. (If desired, reserve a few whole shrimp for garnish.) Set aside.

Meanwhile, cook lasagna noodles according to the directions on page 140. Drain noodles; rinse with cold water. Drain again.

For filling, in a small mixing bowl combine egg, ricotta or cottage cheese, *half* of the Parmesan cheese, and the basil. Set filling aside.

For sauce, in a medium saucepan cook mushrooms and green onion in margarine or butter till tender. Stir in flour, salt, and pepper. Add milk all at once. Cook and stir till thickened and bubbly. Remove from heat. Stir about *1 cup* of the hot mixture into the sour cream; return all the sour cream mixture to the saucepan. Stir fish and shrimp into the sauce.

To assemble, layer *half* of the cooked noodles in a 2-quart rectangular baking dish. Spread with *half* of the filling. Top with *half* of the sauce and *half* of the mozzarella cheese. Repeat layers. Sprinkle with remaining Parmesan cheese.

Bake in a 375° oven for 30 to 35 minutes or till heated through. Let stand 10 minutes before serving. If desired, garnish with reserved whole shrimp and basil leaves. Makes 10 main-dish servings.

Nutrition information per serving: 336 calories, 28 g protein, 16 g carbohydrate, 17 g fat (9 g saturated), 106 mg cholesterol, 441 mg sodium, 388 mg potassium.

SPINACH AND ORZO PIE

Orzo is among the tiniest of pastas. In this dish it provides a nifty crust for the spinach and ricotta filling.

1½ cups packaged dried orzo (9 ounces)
2 beaten eggs
1 15½-ounce jar chunky spaghetti sauce
⅓ cup grated Parmesan cheese
1 10-ounce package frozen chopped
    spinach
½ cup ricotta cheese
¼ teaspoon ground nutmeg
½ cup shredded fontina *or* mozzarella
    cheese (2 ounces)

Cook pasta according to the directions on page 140. Drain pasta; rinse with cold water. Drain again.

In a medium mixing bowl combine eggs, *½ cup* of the spaghetti sauce, and Parmesan cheese. Add pasta; toss to coat. Spread pasta mixture over the bottom and up the sides of a greased 9-inch pie plate to form an even shell; set aside.

Cook spinach according to package directions; drain well. In another mixing bowl stir together spinach, ricotta cheese, and nutmeg. Spoon into bottom of the pasta-lined pie plate. Spread remaining spaghetti sauce over the filling. Cover edge of pie with foil.

Bake in a 350° oven for 30 minutes. Sprinkle with fontina or mozzarella cheese. Bake for 3 to 5 minutes more or till cheese melts. Let stand 5 minutes before serving. Cut into wedges. Makes 6 main-dish servings.

Nutrition information per serving: 374 calories, 17 g protein, 49 g carbohydrate, 12 g fat (5 g saturated), 93 mg cholesterol, 617 mg sodium, 471 mg potassium.

BAKED FONTINA FETTUCCINE

Fontina cheese, a semi-soft Italian cheese, gives a pleasant nutty flavor to this crusty baked pasta dish.

8   ounces packaged dried fettuccine,
      broken
1   cup boiling water
½   cup snipped dried tomatoes
      (not oil-packed)
1½ cups shredded fontina *or* Gruyère
      cheese (6 ounces)
⅔   cup whipping cream
¼   cup grated Parmesan *or* Romano
      cheese
2   tablespoons margarine *or* butter
⅛   teaspoon pepper
1   tablespoon margarine *or* butter
⅓   cup fine dry bread crumbs
      Fresh rosemary (optional)
      Dried tomatoes (not oil-packed)
        (optional)
      Fresh rosemary sprigs (optional)

Cook pasta according to the directions on page 140. Drain pasta; rinse with cold water. Drain again.

Meanwhile, pour the boiling water over the snipped dried tomatoes. Let stand for 2 minutes; drain.

In a large mixing bowl combine the pasta, the rehydrated snipped tomatoes, fontina or Gruyère cheese, whipping cream, Parmesan or Romano cheese, 2 tablespoons margarine or butter, and pepper. Toss till well mixed.

Use the 1 tablespoon margarine or butter to generously grease an 8x1½-inch round baking pan. Sprinkle with bread crumbs, coating pan evenly. Transfer pasta mixture to the crumb-coated pan.

Bake in a 350° oven for 15 to 20 minutes or till heated through. Let stand for 10 minutes.

Meanwhile, if desired, pour boiling water over additional dried tomatoes. Let stand 2 minutes. Drain; cut tomatoes in half. Set aside.

Invert the baking pan onto a serving platter to unmold. If desired, garnish with rehydrated tomatoes and fresh rosemary. Cut into wedges to serve. Makes 4 main-dish servings.

Nutrition information per serving: 677 calories, 24 g protein, 57 g carbohydrate, 40 g fat (20 g saturated), 109 mg cholesterol, 640 mg sodium, 213 mg potassium.

CHILI MACARONI

Wagon wheel macaroni and green beans replace the kidney beans in this chili-style dish.

12   ounces ground beef *or* ground raw
     turkey
 1   medium onion, chopped (½ cup)
 1   14½-ounce can Mexican-style stewed
     tomatoes
1¼ cups tomato juice
 2   tablespoons canned diced green chili
     peppers, drained
 2   teaspoons chili powder
 ½   teaspoon garlic salt
 1   cup packaged dried wagon wheel
     macaroni *or* elbow macaroni
 1   cup loose-pack frozen cut green beans
 1   cup shredded cheddar cheese
     (4 ounces)

In a large skillet cook ground beef or turkey and onion till meat is brown. Drain fat.

Stir stewed tomatoes, tomato juice, chili peppers, chili powder, and garlic salt into the meat mixture. Bring to boiling. Stir in pasta and green beans. Return to boiling; reduce heat. Cover and simmer about 15 minutes or till pasta and beans are tender.

To serve, spoon into bowls. Sprinkle *each* serving with shredded cheddar cheese. Makes 4 main-dish servings.

Nutrition information per serving: 427 calories, 29 g protein, 32 g carbohydrate, 21 g fat (10 g saturated), 83 mg cholesterol, 1,118 mg sodium, 773 mg potassium.

STOVETOP STROGANOFF

You need only one skillet for this take-off on classic stroganoff.

12 ounces beef tenderloin steak *or* beef
      sirloin steak
 1 tablespoon margarine *or* butter
1½ cups sliced fresh mushrooms
 1 medium onion, cut into thin wedges
 1 clove garlic, minced
 2 cups water
 4 ounces packaged dried mafalda *or*
      fettuccine, broken
 2 teaspoons instant beef bouillon
      granules
 ¼ teaspoon pepper
 1 8-ounce carton dairy sour cream *or*
      plain yogurt
 2 tablespoons all-purpose flour
 1 tablespoon snipped parsley

Trim fat from beef. Partially freeze beef. Thinly slice beef across the grain into bite-size strips.

In a large skillet cook and stir the meat in margarine or butter till meat is brown. Remove meat from skillet; set aside.

Add mushrooms, onion, and garlic to skillet. Cook and stir till vegetables are tender. Stir in water, pasta, bouillon granules, and pepper. Bring to boiling; reduce heat. Cover and simmer about 12 minutes or till pasta is tender, stirring frequently.

Meanwhile, stir together sour cream or yogurt and flour. Stir sour cream mixture and parsley into the pasta mixture. Return beef strips to the skillet. Cook till bubbly, stirring gently. Cook and stir for 1 minute more. Makes 4 main-dish servings.

Nutrition information per serving: 408 calories, 23 g protein, 31 g carbohydrate, 21 g fat (10 g saturated), 73 mg cholesterol, 539 mg sodium, 497 mg potassium.

LAMB STEW WITH BOW TIES

Overflowing with mushrooms, green beans, carrots, and zucchini, this lamb stew makes a great tummy-warmer on blustery nights.

1   pound lamb *or* beef stew meat
2   tablespoons cooking oil
1   medium onion, sliced and separated
       into rings
3   cups water
¼   cup snipped dried tomatoes
       (not oil-packed)
½   teaspoon ground cinnamon
½   teaspoon dried oregano, crushed
¼   teaspoon salt
¼   teaspoon pepper
2   cups sliced fresh mushrooms
1   9-ounce package frozen cut green beans
2   medium carrots, thinly sliced (1 cup)
1   medium zucchini, halved lengthwise
       and cut into 1-inch slices
¾   cup packaged dried medium bow ties
1   15-ounce can herbed tomato sauce

In a Dutch oven or large saucepan cook *half* of the lamb or beef in hot oil till the meat is brown; remove meat. Repeat with remaining meat. Set all the meat aside.

Cook the onion in the drippings till tender. Drain fat. Stir all of the meat, the water, dried tomatoes, cinnamon, oregano, salt, and pepper into the Dutch oven. Bring to boiling; reduce heat. Cover and simmer about 45 minutes for the lamb *or* about 1¼ hours for the beef or till the meat is nearly tender.

Stir mushrooms, green beans, carrots, zucchini, and pasta into the meat mixture. Return to boiling. Cover and simmer about 20 minutes more or till meat, vegetables, and pasta are tender. Stir in the tomato sauce; heat through. Makes 4 main-dish servings.

Nutrition information per serving: 312 calories, 24 g protein, 28 g carbohydrate, 13 g fat (3 g saturated), 67 mg cholesterol, 863 mg sodium, 1,037 mg potassium.

POLISH SAUSAGE AND SPAGHETTI IN BEER

Sausage, caraway seed, and beer add up to a pasta dish with a German twist.

1   pound fully cooked Polish sausage *or* smoked sausage, cut into 1-inch pieces
1   cup sliced fresh mushrooms
2   stalks celery, sliced (1 cup)
1   large green pepper, cut into 1-inch pieces
1   medium onion, chopped (½ cup)
1   cup beer
½   cup water
1   8-ounce can tomato sauce
2   tablespoons snipped parsley
½   teaspoon sugar
½   teaspoon caraway seed
4   ounces packaged dried spaghetti, broken into 2-inch pieces
    Grated Parmesan cheese (optional)

In a Dutch oven or a large saucepan cook the sausage till light brown. Remove sausage from Dutch oven; set aside.

Add mushrooms, celery, green pepper, and onion to Dutch oven. Cook and stir about 3 minutes or till vegetables are tender. Stir in beer, water, tomato sauce, parsley, sugar, and caraway seed. Bring to boiling; reduce heat. Cover and simmer for 20 minutes.

Stir in spaghetti. Return to boiling; reduce heat. Cover and simmer for 10 to 12 minutes more or till spaghetti is tender. Add sausage; heat through. Serve in bowls and, if desired, pass Parmesan cheese. Makes 4 main-dish servings.

Nutrition information per serving: 549 calories, 22 g protein, 36 g carbohydrate, 33 g fat (12 g saturated), 79 mg cholesterol, 1,370 mg sodium, 747 mg potassium.

HAM, PASTA, AND BEAN SOUP

For the broth, use either canned chicken broth or dissolve 2 teaspoons instant chicken bouillon granules in 2 cups of boiling water.

1 15-ounce can navy beans, rinsed and drained
2½ cups water
2 cups chicken broth
½ teaspoon dried marjoram *or* basil, crushed
¼ teaspoon pepper
1 cup packaged dried tricolor wagon wheel macaroni *or* elbow macaroni
1 cup cubed fully cooked ham *or* fully cooked smoked turkey
1 medium onion, chopped (½ cup)
1 stalk celery, sliced (½ cup)

Using a potato masher, mash about *half* of the navy beans. Set whole and mashed navy beans aside.

In a large saucepan combine water, chicken broth, marjoram or basil, and pepper. Bring to boiling. Add the mashed and whole navy beans, pasta, ham or smoked turkey, onion, and celery to the broth mixture. Return to boiling; reduce heat. Simmer, uncovered, for 10 to 15 minutes or till pasta is tender but slightly firm, stirring occasionally. Makes 4 main-dish servings.

Nutrition information per serving: 275 calories, 21 g protein, 40 g carbohydrate, 3 g fat (1 g saturated), 11 mg cholesterol, 1,090 mg sodium, 606 mg potassium.

MINESTRONE

Fennel imparts a licoricelike taste to this Italian vegetable soup.

2   medium onions, chopped (1 cup)
1   stalk celery, sliced (½ cup)
1   medium carrot, coarsely chopped
       (½ cup)
2   cloves garlic, minced
¼   teaspoon crushed red pepper
2   tablespoons olive oil *or* cooking oil
2   14½-ounce cans chicken *or* beef broth
1   16-ounce can tomatoes, cut up
1   cup tomato juice
1   small head fennel, halved lengthwise
       and thinly sliced, *or* 1 cup shredded
       cabbage
1   teaspoon dried Italian seasoning,
       crushed
1   15-ounce can cannellini *or* great
       northern beans, rinsed and drained
1   medium zucchini, halved lengthwise
       and sliced ¼ inch thick (1 cup)
½   of a 9-ounce package frozen Italian-
       style green beans *or* cut green beans
¾   cup packaged dried tiny bow ties, small
       shells, *or* other small pasta
½   cup diced prosciutto *or* fully cooked
       ham (2 ounces)
¼   cup grated Parmesan cheese

In a large Dutch oven or kettle cook onions, celery, carrot, garlic, and crushed red pepper in hot olive oil or cooking oil till onion is tender but not brown.

Stir in the chicken or beef broth, *undrained* tomatoes, tomato juice, fennel or cabbage, and Italian seasoning. Bring to boiling; reduce heat. Cover and simmer for 20 minutes.

Stir in the cannellini or great northern beans, zucchini, green beans, pasta, and prosciutto or ham. Bring to boiling; reduce heat. Cover and simmer for 10 to 15 minutes or till vegetables and pasta are tender.

To serve, ladle soup into bowls; sprinkle with Parmesan cheese. Makes 5 main-dish servings.

Nutrition information per serving: 368 calories, 20 g protein, 48 g carbohydrate, 12 g fat (2 g saturated), 4 mg cholesterol, 1,176 mg sodium, 1,076 mg potassium.

SAUSAGE AND PASTA SOUP

The flavorful smoked sausage makes this quick and easy soup taste as if it simmered all day.

5   cups chicken broth
8   ounces fully cooked Polish sausage *or*
     smoked sausage, halved lengthwise
     and cut into ½ inch thick slices
1   medium onion, chopped (½ cup)
1   stalk celery, chopped (½ cup)
2   bay leaves
¼   teaspoon pepper
¾   cup packaged dried tiny tube macaroni
     (ditalini) *or* other small pasta
1   medium yellow summer squash *or*
     zucchini, halved lengthwise and cut
     into ½ inch thick slices (1¼ cups)
1   cup frozen peas

In a large saucepan combine chicken broth, sausage, onion, celery, bay leaves, and pepper. Bring to boiling; reduce heat. Cover and simmer for 20 minutes. Remove bay leaves.

Add pasta, summer squash or zucchini, and peas to broth mixture. Bring to boiling; reduce heat. Simmer, uncovered, for 7 to 9 minutes or till pasta and vegetables are tender. Makes 4 main-dish servings.

Nutrition information per serving: 379 calories, 20 g protein, 31 g carbohydrate, 19 g fat (6 g saturated), 40 mg cholesterol, 1,483 mg sodium, 710 mg potassium.

SAUCY CHICKEN RIGATONI

While cooking this saucepan dinner, stir every now and then, to prevent the pasta from sticking to the pan.

1   medium onion, chopped (½ cup)
1   clove garlic, minced
1   tablespoon cooking oil
1   16-ounce can tomatoes, cut up
1   7½-ounce can tomatoes, cut up
2   cups packaged dried rigatoni *or* elbow
    macaroni
1¼ cups water
1   2½-ounce jar sliced mushrooms,
    drained
1   teaspoon dried Italian seasoning,
    crushed
⅛   teaspoon ground red pepper (optional)
1½ cups chopped cooked chicken *or* turkey
    (about 8 ounces)
    Fresh basil leaves (optional)

In a large saucepan cook onion and garlic in hot oil till tender but not brown. Stir in *undrained* tomatoes, pasta, water, mushrooms, Italian seasoning, and, if desired, ground red pepper. Bring to boiling; reduce heat. Cover and simmer about 20 minutes or till pasta is tender but slightly firm, stirring occasionally.

Stir in chicken or turkey; heat through. If desired, garnish with fresh basil leaves. Makes 4 main-dish servings.

Nutrition information per serving: 293 calories, 22 g protein, 32 g carbohydrate, 9 g fat (2 g saturated), 51 mg cholesterol, 399 mg sodium, 590 mg potassium.

FISH AND SHELL STEW

To vary the flavor, try switching to Cajun-style or Mexican-style stewed tomatoes.

12 ounces fresh *or* frozen skinless fish
       fillets (cod, pike, *or* orange roughy)
 2 14½-ounce cans chicken broth
 1 15-ounce can garbanzo beans *or* red
       kidney beans, rinsed and drained
 1 cup loose-pack frozen mixed vegetables
 ¾ cup packaged dried medium shell
       macaroni *or* cavatelli
 1 medium onion, chopped (½ cup)
 1 teaspoon dried basil *or* thyme, crushed
 ¼ teaspoon pepper
 1 14½-ounce can Italian-style stewed
       tomatoes

Thaw fish, if frozen. Cut fish into 1-inch pieces; set aside.

In a large saucepan stir together broth, beans, frozen vegetables, pasta, onion, basil or thyme, and pepper. Bring to boiling; reduce heat. Cover and simmer for 10 minutes.

Stir in *undrained* tomatoes and fish. Return to boiling; reduce heat. Cover and simmer for 2 to 3 minutes or till fish just begins to flake easily. Makes 4 main-dish servings.

Nutrition information per serving: 291 calories, 26 g protein, 39 g carbohydrate, 4 g fat (1 g saturated), 34 mg cholesterol, 1,261 mg sodium, 839 mg potassium.

BEEF AND ARTICHOKE PASTA SALAD

Main-dish salads, such as this artful combination of beef, artichoke hearts, cheese, olives, and roasted red peppers, are great make-ahead suppers.

4   ounces packaged dried tricolor, spinach, *or* plain corkscrew macaroni
1   14-ounce can artichoke hearts, drained and cut up
1   cup chopped cooked beef (5 ounces)
1   medium red onion, chopped (½ cup)
½   cup bottled roasted sweet red peppers, drained and cut into strips, *or* one 4-ounce jar sliced pimiento, drained
2   ounces provolone *and/or* cheddar cheese, cut into cubes
⅓   cup white wine vinegar *or* white vinegar
¼   cup salad oil
2   tablespoons honey
1   teaspoon dried dillweed
½   teaspoon garlic powder
½   teaspoon pepper
¼   teaspoon salt
4   cups shredded fresh spinach
    Whole spinach leaves (optional)

Cook the pasta according to the directions on page 140. Drain pasta; rinse with cold water. Drain again.

In a large mixing bowl combine pasta, artichoke hearts, beef, onion, roasted peppers or pimiento, and cheese. Toss to mix.

For dressing, in a screw-top jar combine vinegar, oil, honey, dillweed, garlic powder, pepper, and salt. Cover and shake well. Pour dressing over pasta mixture; toss to coat. Cover and chill for 3 to 24 hours.

To serve, line individual plates with shredded spinach. If desired, add a few whole spinach leaves to each plate. Spoon pasta mixture over spinach. Makes 4 main-dish servings.

Nutrition information per serving: 511 calories, 19 g protein, 43 g carbohydrate, 31 g fat (10 g saturated), 45 mg cholesterol, 419 mg sodium, 751 mg potassium.

BEEF AND PASTA SALAD WITH CREAMY GARLIC DRESSING

Another time, substitute frozen cut asparagus for the green beans.

1   cup packaged dried corkscrew
    macaroni *or* cavatelli
1   cup fresh green beans cut into 2-inch
    lengths *or* ½ of a 9-ounce package
    frozen cut green beans
8   ounces cooked beef, cut into thin strips
    (1½ cups)
1   medium red onion, chopped (½ cup)
1   medium carrot, shredded (½ cup)
½   cup sliced radishes
½   cup mayonnaise *or* salad dressing
½   cup plain yogurt
2   teaspoons white wine vinegar *or*
    vinegar
2   cloves garlic, minced
½   teaspoon dried Italian seasoning,
    crushed
¼   teaspoon dry mustard
¼   teaspoon salt
1   to 2 tablespoons milk (optional)
    Salad savoy leaves (optional)

Cook pasta according to the directions on page 140. Drain pasta. Rinse with cold water; drain again.

Meanwhile, cook the green beans in a small amount of boiling salted water for 20 to 25 minutes or till crisp-tender. (If using frozen green beans, cook for 5 to 10 minutes or till crisp-tender.) Drain beans. Rinse with cold water; drain again.

In a large mixing bowl combine pasta, green beans, beef, onion, carrot, and radishes.

For dressing, in a small mixing bowl stir together mayonnaise or salad dressing, yogurt, vinegar, garlic, Italian seasoning, dry mustard, and salt. Pour dressing over pasta mixture. Toss to coat. Cover and chill for 4 to 24 hours.

If necessary, stir milk into the pasta mixture before serving. If desired, serve with salad savoy leaves. Makes 4 main-dish servings.

Nutrition information per serving: 556 calories, 18 g protein, 25 g carbohydrate, 43 g fat (12 g saturated), 70 mg cholesterol, 360 mg sodium, 362 mg potassium.

ALL-AMERICAN HAM AND MACARONI SALAD

Chock full of ham and Monterey Jack cheese, this cool and creamy salad is perfect for a potluck picnic.

1 cup packaged dried wagon wheel *or* elbow macaroni

1½ cups cubed fully cooked ham (8 ounces)

4 ounces Monterey Jack *or* cheddar cheese, cut into cubes (1 cup)

1 cup frozen peas

1 stalk celery, thinly sliced (½ cup)

¼ cup finely chopped onion

2 tablespoons diced pimiento

½ cup mayonnaise *or* salad dressing

¼ cup sweet pickle relish *or* chopped sweet pickle

1 to 2 tablespoons milk (optional)

Dash pepper

8 cherry tomatoes, halved

Fresh parsley sprig (optional)

Cook pasta according to the directions on page 140. Drain pasta; rinse with cold water. Drain again.

In a large mixing bowl combine pasta, ham, cheese, peas, celery, onion, and pimiento. Toss gently to mix.

For dressing, in a small mixing bowl stir together mayonnaise or salad dressing, pickle relish or chopped pickle, milk, and pepper. Pour dressing over pasta mixture. Toss to coat. Cover and chill for 4 to 24 hours.

Just before serving, stir in milk, if necessary. Spoon pasta mixture into a serving bowl.

Arrange cherry tomato halves around the edge of bowl. If desired, garnish with parsley. Makes 4 main-dish servings.

Nutrition information per serving: 534 calories, 25 g protein, 32 g carbohydrate, 34 g fat (10 g saturated), 71 mg cholesterol, 1,175 mg sodium, 455 mg potassium.

HAM, PECAN, AND BLUE CHEESE PASTA SALAD

For a showstopping yet simple salad, toss together this playful combo.

4   ounces fully cooked ham, cut into thin
        bite-size strips
1   cup broken pecans, toasted
½   to ¾ cup crumbled blue cheese (2 to
        3 ounces)
⅓   cup snipped parsley
¼   cup olive oil *or* salad oil
2   tablespoons snipped fresh rosemary *or*
        1 teaspoon dried rosemary, crushed
1   clove garlic, minced
½   teaspoon coarsely ground pepper
8   ounces packaged dried bow ties
        (3½ cups)
    Lettuce leaves (optional)

In a very large mixing bowl combine ham, pecans, blue cheese, parsley, oil, rosemary, garlic, and pepper. Cover and let stand at room temperature for 30 minutes.

Meanwhile, cook pasta according to the directions on page 140. Drain pasta; rinse with cold water. Drain again.

Add pasta to the ham mixture; toss to mix.

If desired, line individual salad plates with lettuce. Divide the pasta mixture among the lettuce-lined plates. Makes 5 main-dish servings.

Nutrition information per serving: 488 calories, 15 g protein, 40 g carbohydrate, 31 g fat (5 g saturated), 15 mg cholesterol, 419 mg sodium, 261 mg potassium.

ORIENTAL CHICKEN PASTA SALAD

Bright chunks of sweet red pepper add a festive note to this sesame-flavored salad.

8   ounces packaged dried square
     spaghetti, spaghetti, *or* linguine
½   of an 8-ounce package frozen baby
     corn *or* one 8¾-ounce can baby
     corn, drained
1½   cups chopped cooked chicken
     (8 ounces)
1   small cucumber, thinly bias-sliced
1   small red sweet *or* green pepper, cut
     into bite-size strips
1   medium carrot, thinly bias-sliced
     (½ cup)
2   green onions, thinly sliced (¼ cup)
⅓   cup tarragon vinegar *or* rice vinegar
¼   cup olive oil *or* salad oil
3   tablespoons soy sauce
1   teaspoon toasted sesame oil
½   teaspoon sugar
½   teaspoon dry mustard
     Dash bottled hot pepper sauce
     Fresh cilantro sprigs (optional)

Cook pasta according to the directions on page 140. Drain pasta; rinse with cold water. Drain again.

If using frozen corn, cook according to package directions. Drain corn; rinse with cold water. Drain again.

In a large mixing bowl combine pasta, corn, chicken, cucumber, red sweet or green pepper, carrot, and green onions. Toss gently to mix.

For dressing, in a screw-top jar combine vinegar, olive or salad oil, soy sauce, sesame oil, sugar, mustard, and bottled hot pepper sauce. Cover and shake well. Pour dressing over the pasta mixture. Toss to coat. Cover and chill for 2 to 24 hours.

To serve, gently toss pasta mixture. Serve on individual salad plates. If desired, garnish with fresh cilantro. Makes 4 main-dish servings.

Nutrition information per serving: 501 calories, 26 g protein, 54 g carbohydrate, 20 g fat (3 g saturated), 51 mg cholesterol, 834 mg sodium, 552 mg potassium.

TURKEY AND FRUIT PASTA SALAD

Savor this refreshing honey-dressed salad in the summertime when nectarines are at their peak.

1   cup packaged dried rope macaroni
     (gemelli) *or* 1⅓ cups corkscrew
     macaroni (4 ounces)

1½ cups chopped cooked turkey *or* chicken
     or fully cooked turkey ham
     (8 ounces)

2   green onions, sliced (¼ cup)

⅓   cup lime *or* lemon juice

¼   cup salad oil

1   tablespoon honey

2   teaspoons snipped fresh thyme *or*
     ½ teaspoon dried thyme, crushed

2   medium nectarines *or* plums, sliced

1   cup halved fresh strawberries

Cook pasta according to the directions on page 140. Drain pasta; rinse with cold water. Drain again.

In a large mixing bowl combine pasta; turkey, chicken, or turkey ham; and green onions. Toss to mix.

For dressing, in a screw-top jar combine lime or lemon juice, oil, honey, and thyme. Cover and shake well. Pour dressing over pasta mixture; toss to coat. Cover and chill for 4 to 24 hours.

Just before serving, stir in nectarines or plums and strawberries. Toss to mix. Makes 4 main-dish servings.

Nutrition information per serving: 393 calories, 21 g protein, 39 g carbohydrate, 17 g fat (3 g saturated), 43 mg cholesterol, 42 mg sodium, 431 mg potassium.

CURRIED PASTA AND CHICKEN SALAD

Yogurt gives just the right amount of tang to the spicy dressing.

2	ounces packaged dried elbow macaroni *or* tiny tube macaroni (ditalini)
1½	cups chopped cooked chicken (about 8 ounces)
1	cup coarsely chopped apple
⅓	cup chopped celery
¼	cup finely chopped onion
⅓	cup mayonnaise *or* salad dressing
⅓	cup plain yogurt
½	teaspoon curry powder
⅛	teaspoon salt
¼	cup cashews *or* peanuts
1	to 2 tablespoons milk (optional)
	Lettuce leaves (optional)

Cook pasta according to the directions on page 140. Drain pasta; rinse with cold water. Drain again.

In a large mixing bowl combine cooked pasta, chicken, apple, celery, and onion.

For dressing, in a small mixing bowl stir together mayonnaise or salad dressing, yogurt, curry powder, and salt. Pour dressing over pasta mixture. Toss to coat. Cover and chill for 4 to 24 hours.

Just before serving, stir cashews or peanuts into pasta mixture. If necessary, stir in milk. If desired, serve salad in lettuce-lined bowls. Makes 4 main-dish serving.

Nutrition information per serving: 376 calories, 21 g protein, 21 g carbohydrate, 23 g fat (4 g saturated), 63 mg cholesterol, 244 mg sodium, 324 mg potassium.

SMOKED TURKEY AND PASTA SALAD

A honey-mustard dressing coats the pasta, smoked chicken, Muenster cheese, and cucumber.

1½ cups packaged dried tricolor *or* plain corkscrew macaroni (4 ounces)

6 ounces Muenster, Swiss, *or* cheddar cheese, cut into cubes (1½ cups)

5 ounces fully cooked smoked turkey breast *or* fully cooked ham, cut into bite-size strips (1 cup)

1 small cucumber, coarsely chopped (1 cup)

½ cup coarsely chopped red sweet *or* green pepper

2 green onions, sliced (¼ cup)

⅓ cup mayonnaise *or* salad dressing

⅓ cup dairy sour cream *or* plain yogurt

1 tablespoon honey

1 tablespoon Dijon-style mustard

¼ teaspoon pepper

1 to 2 tablespoons milk (optional)
Lettuce leaves (optional)

Cook pasta according to the directions on page 140. Drain pasta; rinse with cold water. Drain again.

In a large mixing bowl combine cooked pasta, cheese, smoked turkey or ham, cucumber, red sweet or green pepper, and green onions.

For dressing, in a small mixing bowl stir together mayonnaise or salad dressing, sour cream or yogurt, honey, mustard, and pepper. Pour dressing over pasta mixture. Toss to coat. Cover and chill for 4 to 24 hours.

If necessary, stir milk into pasta mixture before serving. If desired, line individual salad plates with lettuce leaves. Serve pasta mixturre on lettuce-line plates. Makes 4 main-dish servings.

Nutrition information per serving: 525 calories, 22 g protein, 30 g carbohydrate, 36 g fat (13 g saturated), 60 mg cholesterol, 478 mg sodium, 215 mg potassium.

SHRIMP AND PASTA SALAD WITH CAPER DRESSING

Cool and refreshing, serve this truly upscale salad to summertime company.

1 cup packaged dried medium shell macaroni

12 ounces fresh *or* frozen peeled and deveined shrimp

1 large red sweet *or* green pepper, cut into 1-inch squares (1 cup)

2 green onions, sliced (¼ cup)

3 tablespoons white wine vinegar *or* white vinegar

2 tablespoons olive oil *or* salad oil

2 tablespoons capers, drained

2 teaspoons snipped fresh dill *or* ½ teaspoon dried dillweed

1 clove garlic, minced

¼ teaspoon salt

¼ teaspoon pepper

1 cup fresh pea pods *or* ½ of a 6-ounce package frozen pea pods, thawed

Spinach *or* lettuce leaves (optional)

Cook pasta according to the directions on page 140. Drain pasta; rinse with cold water. Drain again.

Meanwhile, cook shrimp, uncovered, in boiling water for 1 to 3 minutes or till shrimp turn pink, stirring occasionally. Drain shrimp; rinse with cold water. Drain again.

In a large mixing bowl combine pasta, shrimp, red sweet or green pepper, and green onions. Toss to mix.

For dressing, in a screw-top jar combine vinegar, oil, capers, dill or dillweed, garlic, salt, and pepper. Cover and shake well. Pour dressing over pasta mixture. Toss gently to coat. Cover and chill for 3 to 24 hours.

Just before serving, cut the pea pods in half crosswise. Stir pea pods into pasta mixture. If desired, serve on spinach- or lettuce-lined plates. Makes 4 main-dish servings.

Nutrition information per serving: 231 calories, 18 g protein, 22 g carbohydrate, 8 g fat (1 g saturated), 131 mg cholesterol, 357 mg sodium, 271 mg potassium.

GREEK-STYLE PASTA SALAD

The tangy vinaigrette, flavored with mint and oregano, tastes great on a simple salad of tossed greens, too.

4 ounces packaged dried bow ties *or* elbow macaroni
1 medium cucumber, quartered lengthwise, seeded, and cut into ½-inch thick slices
¼ cup chopped red onion
¼ cup sliced pitted ripe olives
¼ cup olive oil *or* cooking oil
¼ cup lemon juice
1 tablespoon snipped fresh oregano *or* 1 teaspoon dried oregano, crushed
1 tablespoon snipped fresh mint *or* ½ teaspoon dried mint, crushed
¼ teaspoon pepper
   Lettuce leaves (optional)
1 6½-ounce can chunk white tuna (water pack), chilled
1 cup crumbled feta cheese (4 ounces)
6 cherry tomatoes, halved

Cook pasta according to the directions on page 140. Drain pasta; rinse with cold water. Drain again.

In a large mixing bowl combine cooked pasta, cucumber, red onion, and olives. Toss lightly to mix.

For dressing, in a screw-top jar combine oil, lemon juice, oregano, mint, and pepper. Cover and shake well. Pour dressing over pasta mixture. Toss to coat. Cover and chill for 4 to 24 hours.

If desired, line individual salad plates with lettuce. Spoon pasta mixture onto the lettuce-lined plates. Drain tuna and break into chunks. Arrange tuna and feta cheese on top of the pasta mixture. Garnish with cherry tomatoes. Makes 4 main-dish servings.

Nutrition information per serving: 289 calories, 21 g protein, 29 g carbohydrate, 10 g fat (5 g saturated), 44 mg cholesterol, 540 mg sodium, 397 mg potassium.

LENTIL SALAD WITH PASTA SHELLS

A refreshingly zippy mustard dressing perks up this meatless main-course salad.

½ cup dry lentils
1½ cups water
¼ teaspoon salt
6 ounces packaged dried small shell
   macaroni (2 cups)
¾ cup chopped broccoli
½ cup chopped, seeded cucumber
¼ cup chopped green pepper
1 green onion, sliced (2 tablespoons)
½ cup plain yogurt
1 tablespoon snipped parsley
1 tablespoon milk
2 to 3 teaspoons Dijon-style mustard
1 teaspoon sugar
¼ teaspoon salt
¼ teaspoon pepper
2 small tomatoes
1 to 2 tablespoons milk (optional)
3 cups shredded lettuce

Rinse and drain lentils. In a small saucepan combine lentils, water, and ¼ teaspoon salt. Bring to boiling; reduce heat. Cover and simmer for 15 to 20 minutes or till the lentils are tender. Drain lentils; rinse with cold water. Drain again.

Cook pasta according to the directions on page 140. Drain pasta; rinse with cold water. Drain again.

In a large mixing bowl combine lentils, pasta, broccoli, cucumber, green pepper, and green onion. Toss to mix.

For dressing, in a small mixing bowl stir together yogurt, parsley, 1 tablespoon milk, mustard, sugar, ¼ teaspoon salt, and pepper. Pour over lentil mixture. Toss to coat. Cover and chill for 2 to 24 hours.

To serve, cut *one* of the tomatoes in half crosswise; chop *one* of the tomato halves. Stir chopped tomato into lentil mixture. If necessary, stir 1 to 2 tablespoons milk into lentil mixture.

Line individual salad plates with lettuce. Cut the remaining tomato half and the whole tomato into slices. Then cut the tomato slices in half. Divide tomatoes among the lettuce-lined plates. Spoon lentil mixture over the tomatoes. Makes 4 main-dish servings.

Nutrition information per serving: 310 calories, 16 g protein, 58 g carbohydrate, 2 g fat (1 g saturated), 2 mg cholesterol, 589 mg sodium, 675 mg potassium.

FRESH TOMATO SOUP WITH TORTELLINI

Pasta and garden-fresh tomatoes are natural go-togethers. Here, they meet in a sage-scented soup.

1 large onion, chopped (1 cup)
2 tablespoons margarine *or* butter
2 pounds ripe tomatoes (about
    6 medium), peeled, seeded,
    and chopped
3 cups chicken broth
1 8-ounce can tomato sauce
1 tablespoon snipped fresh sage *or*
    1 teaspoon dried sage, crushed
¼ teaspoon salt
   Dash pepper
4 ounces packaged dried tortellini
¼ cup finely shredded *or* grated Parmesan
    cheese
   Fresh sage leaves (optional)

In a large saucepan cook onion in margarine or butter till tender. Add tomatoes, chicken broth, tomato sauce, sage, salt, and pepper. Bring to boiling; reduce heat. Cover and simmer for 30 minutes. Cool slightly.

Meanwhile, cook tortellini according to directions on page 140; drain.

Press tomato mixture through a food mill. (*Or,* place *one-third to one-half* of the mixture in a blender container or food processor bowl. Cover and blend or process till smooth. Repeat with remaining mixture.)

Return tomato mixture to saucepan. Add cooked and drained tortellini; heat through. Spoon soup into bowls; sprinkle with Parmesan cheese. If desired, garnish with fresh sage leaves. Makes 6 side-dish servings or 4 main-dish servings.

Nutrition information per serving: 196 calories, 10 g protein, 24 g carbohydrate, 7 g fat (2 g saturated), 16 mg cholesterol, 957 mg sodium, 677 mg potassium.

LEMON-BASIL PASTA WITH VEGETABLES

Most grocery stores stock several combinations of loose-pack frozen vegetables. Choose the one that strikes your fancy.

1 cup packaged dried orecchietti, medium shell macaroni, corkscrew macaroni, *or* bow ties

1½ cups loose-pack frozen mixed broccoli, French-style green beans, onions, and red sweet pepper *or* other vegetable combination

3 tablespoons margarine *or* butter

1 tablespoon snipped parsley

1 clove garlic, minced

1 teaspoon finely shredded lemon peel

½ teaspoon dried basil, crushed

⅛ teaspoon salt

Dash ground red pepper

Cook pasta according to the directions on page 140, adding the frozen vegetables the last 5 minutes of cooking time. Drain.

Meanwhile, in a small saucepan melt the margarine or butter. Stir in parsley, garlic, lemon peel, basil, salt, and ground red pepper. Pour over pasta mixture. Toss to coat. Makes 4 side-dish servings.

Nutrition information per serving: 178 calories, 4 g protein, 20 g carbohydrate, 9 g fat (2 g saturated), 0 mg cholesterol, 176 mg sodium, 130 mg potassium.

PASTA WITH RED PEPPER SAUCE

Roasted red peppers, white wine, and sour cream make a colorful sauce that dresses up any pasta.

10   ounces packaged dried plain *or* spinach
         fettuccine *or* linguine
  2   large red sweet peppers, roasted*, *or*
         one 12-ounce jar roasted red sweet
         peppers, drained
  ¾   cup dairy sour cream
  2   tablespoons dry white wine
  ½   teaspoon salt
  ⅛   teaspoon pepper
         Roasted* red sweet pepper strips
            (optional)

Cook pasta according to the directions on page 140. Drain; keep warm.

Meanwhile, for sauce, in a food processor or blender container, place the 2 roasted peppers. Process or blend till smooth.

In a small saucepan heat the pureed peppers over medium-low heat for 2 to 3 minutes or till bubbly. Gradually stir in the sour cream, wine, salt, and pepper. Heat through, but do not boil.

Arrange the pasta on individual plates. Spoon the sauce over the pasta. If desired, garnish with roasted red sweet pepper strips. Makes 8 side-dish servings.

To Roast Peppers: Quarter the peppers. Then remove and discard stems, seeds, and membranes. Place peppers, cut side down, on a foil-lined baking sheet. Bake in a 425° oven for 20 to 25 minutes or till skins are blistered and dark. Remove from baking sheet. Immediately place in a paper bag. Close bag; let stand about 30 minutes to steam the peppers so the skins peel away more easily. Using a sharp knife, remove skins from peppers, pulling skins off in strips. Discard skins.

Nutrition information per serving: 184 calories, 5 g protein, 28 g carbohydrate, 5 g fat (3 g saturated), 10 mg cholesterol, 159 mg sodium, 123 mg potassium.

FUSILLI WITH PESTO

This recipe makes enough pesto for three meals. Chill or freeze the remaining pesto.

1 cup firmly packed fresh basil leaves
½ cup firmly packed parsley sprigs with
   stems removed
½ cup grated Parmesan *or* Romano cheese
¼ cup olive oil *or* cooking oil
¼ cup pine nuts, walnuts, *or* almonds
1 large clove garlic, sliced
¼ teaspoon salt
4 ounces packaged dried fusilli,
   spaghetti, *or* other pasta
   Finely shredded *or* grated Parmesan
   cheese (optional)

For pesto, in a blender container or food processor bowl combine basil, parsley, Parmesan or Romano cheese, oil, nuts, garlic, and salt. Cover and blend or process with several on-off turns till a paste forms, stopping the machine several times and scraping the sides.

To serve, cook pasta according to the directions on page 140. Drain. Add about *one-third* of the pesto to the pasta; toss to coat. If desired, sprinkle with Parmesan cheese.

Store remaining pesto in airtight containers. Chill up to 2 days or freeze up to 1 month. Bring pesto to room temperature before tossing with pasta. Makes 4 side-dish servings. Makes ¾ cup pesto (enough for 12 side-dish servings).

Nutrition information per serving: 190 calories, 7 g protein, 24 g carbohydrate, 8 g fat (2 g saturated), 3 mg cholesterol, 124 mg sodium, 81 mg potassium.

FETTUCCINE WITH ARTICHOKE SAUCE

Artichoke hearts stirred into an herbed white sauce dresses up fettuccine for a special occasion side dish.

4   ounces packaged dried fettuccine
      or linguine
½   of a medium onion, chopped (¼ cup)
1   clove garlic, minced
1   tablespoon olive oil *or* cooking oil
2   tablespoons all-purpose flour
¼   teaspoon dried basil *or* oregano,
      crushed
⅛   teaspoon salt
1   cup milk
½   of a 14-ounce can artichoke hearts,
      drained and cut up
2   tablespoons grated Parmesan *or*
      Romano cheese
1   tablespoon snipped parsley
1   to 2 tablespoons milk (optional)
    Snipped parsley (optional)
    Coarsely ground pepper (optional)
    Tomato wedges (optional)
    Parsley sprigs (optional)

Cook pasta according to the directions on page 140. Drain.

Meanwhile, for sauce, in a medium saucepan cook onion and garlic in oil till onion is tender. Stir in flour, basil or oregano, and salt. Add 1 cup milk all at once. Cook and stir till thickened and bubbly. Cook and stir for 1 minute more. Stir in artichoke hearts, Parmesan or Romano cheese, and 1 tablespoon parsley; heat through. If necessary, stir in enough additional milk to make of desired consistency.

Spoon pasta onto individual plates or a large platter. Ladle the sauce over the hot pasta. If desired, sprinkle with additional snipped parsley and pepper and garnish with tomato wedges and parsley sprigs. Makes 4 side-dish servings.

Nutrition information per serving: 221 calories, 9 g protein, 33 g carbohydrate, 6 g fat (2 g saturated), 7 mg cholesterol, 254 mg sodium, 264 mg potassium.

SHELLS WITH MASCARPONE CHEESE AND WALNUTS

Look for marcarpone cheese at Italian speciality shops or gourmet shops. This soft, mild-flavored cheese makes this sauce extra creamy.

4　ounces packaged dried tricolor
　　medium shell macaroni *or* cavatelli
　　(1⅓ cups)
2　green onions, sliced (¼ cup)
2　tablespoons margarine *or* butter
½　of an 8-ounce container mascarpone
　　cheese *or* soft-style cream cheese
¼　cup milk
2　tablespoons finely shredded Parmesan
　　cheese
¼　cup coarsely chopped walnuts, toasted

Cook pasta according to the directions on page 140. Drain.

Meanwhile, for sauce, in a medium saucepan cook the green onions in margarine or butter over medium-high heat for 1 minute. Reduce heat. Add the mascarpone or cream cheese. Cook and stir till cheese melts. Add milk and stir till sauce is smooth. Stir in Parmesan cheese.

Pour sauce over pasta; toss to coat. Sprinkle with toasted walnuts. Makes 4 side-dish servings.

Nutrition information per serving: 354 calories, 13 g protein, 26 g carbohydrate, 25 g fat (9 g saturated), 40 mg cholesterol, 132 mg sodium, 95 mg potassium.

ITALIAN-STYLE ZUCCHINI AND PASTA

Fennel seed and crushed red pepper lend Italian flavor to this dish.

½ cup packaged dried cavatelli, medium pasta shells, *or* elbow macaroni

1 large onion, chopped (1 cup)

¼ cup thinly sliced *or* coarsely chopped carrot

1 clove garlic, minced

2 tablespoons olive oil *or* cooking oil

1 14½-ounce can Italian-style stewed tomatoes

1 small zucchini, halved lengthwise and sliced ¼-inch thick

½ teaspoon fennel seed, crushed

⅛ to ¼ teaspoon crushed red pepper

Cook the pasta according to the directions on page 140. Drain.

Meanwhile, in a large skillet cook onion, carrot, and garlic in hot oil for 5 minutes or till tender. Add tomatoes, zucchini, fennel seed, and crushed red pepper. Bring to boiling; reduce heat. Simmer, uncovered, for 3 minutes. Stir in pasta. Heat through. Makes 4 side-dish servings.

Nutrition information per serving: 200 calories, 5 g protein, 30 g carbohydrate, 7 g fat (1 g saturated), 0 mg cholesterol, 370 mg sodium, 529 mg potassium.

ANGEL HAIR PASTA WITH CREAMY MUSHROOM SAUCE

Angel hair pasta, the thinnest pasta strands of all, adds a delicate look to the gently flavored sauce.

4	ounces packaged dried angel hair pasta (capellini)
1½	cups sliced fresh mushrooms
1	medium onion, chopped (½ cup)
1	tablespoon margarine *or* butter
1	3-ounce package cream cheese, cut into cubes
¼	teaspoon salt
⅛	teaspoon pepper
⅓	cup milk
2	tablespoons snipped chives

Cook pasta according to the directions on page 140. Drain.

Meanwhile, for sauce, in a medium saucepan cook the mushrooms and onion in the margarine or butter till vegetables are tender. Stir in cream cheese, salt, and pepper. Cook and stir over low heat till cheese is melted. Gradually stir in milk and chives; heat through.

Pour sauce over pasta. Toss to coat. Serve immediately. Makes 4 side-dish servings.

Nutrition information per serving: 234 calories, 7 g protein, 27 g carbohydrate, 11 g fat (6 g saturated), 25 mg cholesterol, 243 mg sodium, 212 mg potassium.

ZITI WITH BLUE CHEESE SAUCE

This tangy sauced pasta dish tastes great alongside steak or broiled chicken.

1   cup packaged dried cut ziti *or*
       corkscrew macaroni
½   teaspoon salt (optional)
3   cups loose-pack frozen broccoli,
       cauliflower, and carrots
2   tablespoons margarine *or* butter
2   tablespoons all-purpose flour
⅛   teaspoon salt
⅛   teaspoon pepper
1   cup milk
½   cup crumbled blue cheese (2 ounces)
⅓   cup dairy sour cream
       Crumbled blue cheese (optional)

In a large saucepan bring 2 quarts *water* to boiling. Add pasta and, if desired, ½ teaspoon salt. Return to boiling; cook for 5 minutes. Add frozen vegetables. Return to boiling; cook for 5 to 7 minutes more or till pasta is tender but slightly firm and vegetables are crisp-tender. Drain pasta and vegetables.

Meanwhile, for sauce, in a small saucepan melt margarine or butter. Stir in flour, ⅛ teaspoon salt, and pepper. Add milk all at once. Cook and stir till thickened and bubbly. Cook and stir for 1 minute more. Remove from heat. Stir in ½ cup blue cheese and the sour cream.

Pour sauce over pasta mixture. Toss to coat. If desired, sprinkle with additional blue cheese. Makes 6 side-dish servings.

Nutrition information per serving: 223 calories, 8 g protein, 26 g carbohydrate, 10 g fat (5 g saturated), 16 mg cholesterol, 280 mg sodium, 275 mg potassium.

MEDITERRANEAN PASTA SALAD

Toss pasta strands, carrot strips, and olive halves with a basil and garlic viniagrette.

3 ounces packaged dried fettuccine, broken
1 medium carrot, cut into julienne strips
½ of a 6-ounce can pitted ripe olives, halved
2 tablespoons vinegar
1 tablespoon water
1 tablespoon olive oil *or* cooking oil
1 clove garlic, minced
¾ teaspoon dried basil, crushed
½ teaspoon sugar
⅛ teaspoon onion powder
   Dash pepper

In a large saucepan or Dutch oven bring 3 quarts of *water* to boiling. Add pasta; return to boiling. Reduce heat. Boil, uncovered, for 6 minutes. Add carrot strips; cook for 2 to 4 minutes more or till pasta is tender but slightly firm and carrot strips are crisp-tender. Drain pasta and carrot strips; rinse with cold water. Drain again.

In a medium mixing bowl combine pasta mixture and olives.

For dressing, in a screw-top jar combine vinegar, water, oil, garlic, basil, sugar, onion powder, and pepper. Cover and shake well. Pour dressing over pasta mixture. Toss to coat. Cover and chill for 3 to 24 hours, tossing pasta mixture occasionally. Toss again just before serving. Makes 4 side-dish servings.

Nutrition information per serving: 155 calories, 4 g protein, 21 g carbohydrate, 8 g fat (1 g saturated), 0 mg cholesterol, 121 mg sodium, 96 mg potassium.

FUSILLI SALAD WITH HERBED WINE DRESSING

To keep the nuts crunchy, add them just before serving the chilled salad.

¼   cup dry white wine
¾   cup light raisins
4   ounces packaged dried tricolor *or* plain fusilli, broken, *or* corkscrew macaroni
2   tablespoons olive oil *or* salad oil
2   tablespoons lemon juice
1   tablespoon snipped fresh tarragon, basil, *or* chives
1   tablespoon minced shallots *or* chopped green onion
2   teaspoons Dijon-style mustard
¼   teaspoon salt
¼   teaspoon pepper
¾   cup Greek olives *or* ripe olives, pitted and quartered
¼   cup pine nuts *or* broken walnuts, toasted

In a small saucepan heat the wine over medium heat just till warm. Add raisins. Let stand for 15 to 30 minutes to plump. Drain raisins, reserving wine. Set raisins and wine aside.

Cook the pasta according to the directions on page 140. Drain pasta; rinse with cold water. Drain again.

In a large mixing bowl toss together pasta and raisins.

For dressing, in a screw-top jar combine reserved wine; olive or salad oil; lemon juice; tarragon, basil, or chives; shallots or green onion; mustard; salt; and pepper. Cover and shake well. Pour dressing over pasta mixture. Toss to coat. Cover and chill for 3 to 24 hours.

To serve, add olives and nuts to pasta mixture. Toss to mix. Makes 6 side-dish servings.

Nutrition information per serving: 233 calories, 5 g protein, 32 g carbohydrate, 10 g fat (1 g saturated), 0 mg cholesterol, 286 mg sodium, 219 mg potassium.

FLORENTINE PASTA SALAD

Refrigerated pesto sauce becomes a handy dressing for the linguine.

2 ounces packaged dried linguine *or* fettuccine

½ of a 7-ounce package fresh refrigerated pesto sauce

1 tablespoon lemon juice

1 cup shredded fresh spinach

½ cup coarsely chopped, seeded tomato

1 small red onion, thinly sliced (⅓ cup)

2 tablespoons pine nuts *or* slivered almonds, toasted

Cook pasta according to the directions on page 140. Drain pasta; rinse with cold water. Drain again.

In a large mixing bowl combine pesto sauce and lemon juice. Add pasta; toss to coat.

Add spinach, tomato, and red onion to pasta mixture; toss till mixed. Sprinkle with nuts. Serve immediately. Makes 4 side-dish servings.

Nutrition information per serving: 224 calories, 6 g protein, 19 g carbohydrate, 15 g fat (0 g saturated), 2 mg cholesterol, 150 mg sodium, 214 mg potassium.

RUFFLED PASTA WITH WILTED GREENS

A sweet onion, such as a Vidalia or a Walla Walla, makes a tasty addition to this warm salad.

2   cups packaged dried pasta ruffles *or*
        corkscrew macaroni
2   tablespoons water
2   tablespoons dry sherry
2   tablespoons soy sauce
1   tablespoon lemon juice
1   tablespoon honey
1   large red onion, thinly sliced and
        separated into rings
1   tablespoon toasted sesame seed
2   tablespoons sesame oil *or* cooking oil
6   cups torn mixed greens

Cook pasta according to the directions on page 140. Drain pasta; rinse with cold water. Drain again.

Meanwhile, in a small mixing bowl combine water, sherry, soy sauce, lemon juice, and honey. Set aside.

In a large skillet cook onion and sesame seed in hot oil about 5 minutes or till onion is tender and seeds are toasted. Stir in soy mixture. Bring to boiling; remove from heat. Add pasta; toss till coated.

Place greens in a large salad bowl. Pour pasta mixture over greens. Toss to mix. Serve immediately. Makes 6 side-dish servings.

Nutrition information per serving: 188 calories, 5 g protein, 28 g carbohydrate, 6 g fat (1 g saturated), 0 mg cholesterol, 350 mg sodium, 205 mg potassium.

HOMEMADE PASTA

Making pasta from scratch is surprisingly easy and the delicious results are worth the effort. See page 140 for information on substituting Homemade Pasta or fresh refrigerated pasta for packaged dried pasta.

2⅓ **cups all-purpose flour**
 ½ **teaspoon salt**
 2 **beaten eggs**
 ⅓ **cup water**
 1 **teaspoon olive oil** *or* **cooking oil**

In a large mixing bowl stir together 2 cups of the flour and salt. Make a well in the center of the mixture.

In a small mixing bowl stir together eggs, water, and oil. Add to the flour mixture and mix well.

Sprinkle kneading surface with the remaining flour. Turn dough out onto the floured surface. Knead till dough is smooth and elastic (8 to 10 minutes total). Cover and let rest for 10 minutes.

Divide dough into fourths. On a lightly floured surface, roll each fourth into a 12-inch square (about ⅟₁₆ inch thick). Let dough stand for about 20 minutes or till slightly dry. Shape as desired (see tip, opposite).

Or, if using a pasta machine, pass each fourth of dough through machine, according to manufacturer's directions, till ⅟₁₆ inch thick. Shape as desired (see tip, opposite).

Cook pasta (see page 140), allowing a few more minutes for dried or frozen pasta. Drain well. Makes 1 pound fresh pasta (8 servings).

Nutrition information per serving: 146 calories, 5 g protein, 26 g carbohydrate, 2 g fat (1 g saturated), 53 mg cholesterol, 150 mg sodium, 51 mg potassium.

HERB PASTA:

Prepare Homemade Pasta as directed at left, except add 1 teaspoon crushed dried *basil, marjoram,* or *sage* to the flour mixture.

Nutrition information per serving: 146 calories, 5 g protein, 26 g carbohydrate, 2 g fat (1 g saturated), 53 mg cholesterol, 150 mg sodium, 54 mg potassium.

SPINACH PASTA:

Prepare Homemade Pasta as directed at left, *except* reduce water to 3 tablespoons and add ⅓ cup very finely chopped, well-drained, cooked *spinach* to the egg mixture.

Nutrition information per serving: 146 calories, 5 g protein, 26 g carbohydrate, 2 g fat (1 g saturated), 53 mg cholesterol, 152 mg sodium, 64 mg potassium.

WHOLE WHEAT PASTA:

Prepare Homemade Pasta as directed at left, *except* substitute *whole wheat flour* for the all-purpose flour.

Nutrition information per serving: 142 calories, 6 g protein, 26 g carbohydrate, 2 g fat (1 g saturated), 53 mg cholesterol, 151 mg sodium, 157 mg potassium.

SHAPING AND STORING PASTA

Lasagna: Cut dough into strips about 2½ inches wide. Then cut into desired lengths.

Farfalle: Cut into 2x1-inch rectangles. Pinch centers to form bow ties.

Tripolini: Cut into 1-inch circles. Pinch centers, forming butterfly shapes.

Linguine *or* **fettuccine:** After rolling dough and letting it stand, loosely roll up dough jelly-roll style; cut into ⅛-inch wide slices for linguine or ¼-inch wide slices for fettuccine. Shake stands to separate. Cut into desired lengths.

To Store Pasta: After cutting and shaping pasta, spread it on a wire rack or hang it from a pasta drying rack or clothes hanger. Let dry overnight or till completely dry. Place in an airtight container and refrigerate for up to 3 days. *Or,* dry the pasta at least 1 hour. Seal it in a moisture- and vaporproof plastic bag or container. Freeze for up to 8 months.

COOKING PASTA

To cook pasta, you need a large saucepan or Dutch oven and lots of water (about 3 quarts of water for 4 to 8 ounces pasta). Bring the water to boiling over high heat. If desired, add 1 teaspoon salt and 1 tablespoon olive oil or cooking oil to help keep the pasta separated. Add pasta, a little at a time, so water does not stop boiling. (Hold long pasta, such as spaghetti, at one end and dip other end into water. As pasta softens, gently curl it around pan and down into water.) Reduce heat slightly. Boil, uncovered, for time specified or till pasta is al dente (tender but slightly firm). Stir occasionally. Test often for doneness near end of cooking time. Immediately drain in a colander.

In recipes that call for packaged dried pasta, you may substitute 8 ounces homemade pasta or refrigerated pasta for 4 ounces of the dried product.

COOKING HOMEMADE OR FRESH REFRIGERATED PASTA

Bow ties: 2 to 3 minutes

Bow ties (tiny): 2 to 3 minutes

Fettuccine: 1 to 2 minutes

Lasagna: 2 to 3 minutes

Linguine: 1 to 2 minutes

Ravioli: 6 to 8 minutes

Tortellini: 8 to 10 minutes

If homemade pasta is dried or frozen, allow a few more minutes.

COOKING PACKAGED DRIED PASTA

Angel hair pasta: 5 to 6 minutes

Acini de pepe: 5 to 6 minutes

Bow ties: 10 minutes

Bow ties (tiny): 5 to 6 minutes

Cavatelli: 12 minutes

Corkscrew or spiral macaroni: 8 to 10 minutes

Fettuccine: 8 to 10 minutes

Fusilli: 15 minutes

Lasagna: 10 to 12 minutes

Linguine: 8 to 10 minutes

Mafalda: 10 to 12 minutes

Manicotti: 18 minutes

Mostaccioli: 14 minutes

Orecchietti: 9 to 12 minutes

Orzo or Rosamarina: 5 to 8 minutes

Rigatoni: 15 minutes

Shell macaroni (jumbo): 23 to 25 minutes

Shell macaroni (medium or large): 12 to 14 minutes

Shell macaroni (small): 8 to 9 minutes

Spaghetti: 10 to 12 minutes

Spaghetti twists (gemelli): 10 minutes

Spaghettini: 8 to 10 minutes

Tortellini: 15 minutes

Vermicelli: 5 to 7 minutes

Wagon wheel macaroni: 10 to 12 minutes

Ziti: 14 to 15 minutes

Keep track of your daily nutrition needs by using the information we provide at the end of each recipe. We've analyzed the nutritional content of each recipe serving for you. When a recipe gives an ingredient substitution, we used the first choice in the analysis. If it makes a range of servings (such as 4 to 6), we use the smallest number. Ingredients listed as optional weren't included in the calculations.

METRIC COOKING HINTS

By making a few conversions, cooks in Australia, Canada, and the United Kingdom can use the recipes in Better Homes and Gardens® *Pasta* with confidence. The charts on this page provide a guide for converting measurements from the U.S. customary system, which is used throughout this book, to the imperial and metric systems. There also is a conversion table for oven temperatures to accommodate the differences in oven calibrations.

Volume and Weight: Americans traditionally use cup measures for liquid and solid ingredients. The chart (top right) shows the approximate imperial and metric equivalents. If you are accustomed to weighing solid ingredients, here are some helpful approximate equivalents.
- 1 cup butter, caster sugar, or rice = 8 ounces = about 250 grams
- 1 cup flour = 4 ounces = about 125 grams
- 1 cup icing sugar = 5 ounces = about 150 grams

Spoon measures are used for smaller amounts of ingredients. Although the size of the tablespoon varies slightly among countries. However, for practical purposes and for recipes in this book, a straight substitution is all that's necessary.

Measurements made using cups or spoons should always be level, unless stated otherwise.

Product Differences: Most of the ingredients called for in the recipes in this book are available in English-speaking countries. However, some are known by different names. Here are some common American ingredients and their possible counterparts:
- Sugar is granulated or caster sugar.
- Powdered sugar is icing sugar.
- All-purpose flour is plain household flour or white flour. When self-rising flour is used in place of all-purpose flour in a recipe that calls for leavening, omit the leavening agent (baking soda or baking powder) and salt.
- Light corn syrup is golden syrup.
- Cornstarch is cornflour.
- Baking soda is bicarbonate of soda.
- Vanilla is vanilla essence.

USEFUL EQUIVALENTS

⅛ teaspoon = 0.5ml
¼ teaspoon = 1ml
½ teaspoon = 2 ml
1 teaspoon = 5 ml
¼ cup = 2 fluid ounces = 50ml
⅓ cup = 3 fluid ounces = 75ml
½ cup = 4 fluid ounces = 125ml

⅔ cup = 5 fluid ounces = 150ml
¾ cup = 6 fluid ounces = 175ml
1 cup = 8 fluid ounces = 250ml
2 cups = 1 pint
2 pints = 1 litre
½ inch =1 centimetre
1 inch = 2 centimetres

BAKING PAN SIZES

American	Metric
8x1½-inch round baking pan	20x4-centimetre sandwich or cake tin
9x1½-inch round baking pan	23x3.5-centimetre sandwich or cake tin
11x7x1½-inch baking pan	28x18x4-centimetre baking pan
13x9x2-inch baking pan	32.5x23x5-centimetre baking pan
2-quart rectangular baking dish	30x19x5-centimetre baking pan
15x10x1-inch baking pan	38x25.5x2.5-centimetre baking pan (Swiss roll tin)
9-inch pie plate	22x4- or 23x4-centimetre pie plate
7- or 8-inch springform pan	18- or 20-centimetre springform or loose-bottom cake tin
9x5x3-inch loaf pan	23x13x6-centimetre or 2-pound narrow loaf pan or paté tin
1½-quart casserole	1.5-litre casserole
2-quart casserole	2-litre casserole

OVEN TEMPERATURE EQUIVALENTS

Fahrenheit Setting	Celsius Setting*	Gas Setting
300°F	150°C	Gas Mark 2
325°F	160°C	Gas Mark 3
350°F	180°C	Gas Mark 4
375°F	190°C	Gas Mark 5
400°F	200°C	Gas Mark 6
425°F	220°C	Gas Mark 7
450°F	230°C	Gas Mark 8
Broil		Grill

Electric and gas ovens may be calibrated using Celsius. However, increase the Celsius setting 10 to 20 degrees when cooking above 160°C with an electric oven. For convection or forced-air ovens (gas or electric), lower the temperature setting 10°C when cooking at all heat levels.